The 100 Most Important Words

To Guide Your Life and Teach Your Children

ILYNMW Publishing
Atlanta Georgia

Dedication

This book is dedicated to my Bride and the love of my life - Debbie.   I also want to dedicate this book to my children - Hannah, David, Sarah and Jonathan. I am so proud of you guys and I love you no matter what!

ISBN 978-0-9913244-2-2

Contents

Definitions - In order of Appearance in Book:

Intentional - done in a way that is planned or intended

Wisdom - the natural ability to understand things that most other people cannot understand

Character - the way someone thinks, feels, and behaves: someone's personality

Faith -strong belief or trust in someone or something
: belief in the existence of God : strong religious feelings or beliefs

Family -a group of people who are related to each other

Friends -a person who you like and enjoy being with

Fitness -the quality or state of being fit

Hope -to want something to happen or be true and think that it could happen or be true

Grace - unmerited divine assistance given humans for their regeneration or sanctification

Mercy - kind or forgiving treatment of someone who could be treated harshly

Courage - the ability to do something that you know is difficult or dangerous

Love- a feeling of strong or constant affection for a person

Joy - a feeling of great happiness

Peace - a state in which there is no war or fighting

Patient - able to remain calm and not become annoyed when waiting for a long time or when dealing with problems or difficult people

Kindness - the quality or state of being kind

Goodness- the quality or state of being good

Faithful- having or showing true and constant support or loyalty
: deserving trust: keeping your promises or doing what you are supposed to do
: not having sex with someone who is not your wife, husband, girlfriend, or boyfriend

Gentleness - the quality or state of being gentle; ESPECIALLY: mildness of manners or disposition

Self-Control - restraint exercised over one's own impulses, emotions, or desires

Honor - respect that is given to someone who is admired

Integrity - the quality of being honest and fair

Reputation - the common opinion that people have about someone or something: the way in which people think of someone or something

Loyal - having or showing complete and constant support for someone or something

Forgive - to stop feeling anger toward (someone who has done something wrong) : to stop blaming (someone) : to stop feeling anger about (something) : to forgive someone for (something wrong): to stop requiring payment of (money that is owed)

Thoughtful - showing concern for the needs or feelings of other people

Discipline - a way of behaving that shows a willingness to obey rules or orders

Honesty - the quality of being fair and truthful: the quality of being honest

Generosity: the quality of being kind, understanding, and not selfish

Share - to let someone else have or use a part of (something that belongs to you)

Humility - the quality or state of not thinking you are better than other people

Gratitude - a feeling of appreciation or thanks

Encouragement - something that makes someone more determined, hopeful, or confident

Content - pleased and satisfied: not needing more

Perseverance - the quality that allows someone to continue trying to do something even though it is difficult

Flexible -willing to change or to try different things

Change - to make (someone or something) different

Learning - the activity or process of gaining knowledge or skill by studying, practicing, being taught, or experiencing something

Teachable - able and willing to learn

Attitude - the way you think and feel about someone or something

Motivation - the condition of being eager to act or work

Passion - a strong feeling of enthusiasm or excitement for something or about doing something

Responsible - able to be trusted to do what is right or to do the things that are expected or required

Accountable - required to be responsible for something

Commitment - a promise to do or give something

Respect - a feeling or understanding that someone or something is important, serious, etc., and should be treated in an appropriate way

Obedient - willing to do what someone tells you to do or to follow a law, rule, etc. : willing to obey

Sowing - to plant seeds in an area of ground

Reaping - to get (something, such as a reward) as a result of something that you have done

Choice - the act of choosing: the act of picking or deciding between two or more possibilities

Consequences - something that happens as a result of a particular action or set of conditions

H.A.L.T - Hungry - Angry - Lonely - Tired

Temptation - something that causes a strong urge or desire to have or do something and especially something that is bad, wrong, or unwise

Trial - a test of the quality, value, or usefulness of something

Distraction - something that makes it difficult to think or pay attention

Guard - a state in which someone is carefully looking for possible danger, threats, problems, etc.

Flee - to run away from danger

Fear - to be afraid of (something or someone)

Bold - not afraid of danger or difficult situations

Truth - the real facts about something: the things that are true

Unity - the state of being in full agreement

Worship - the act of showing respect and love for a god especially by praying with other people who believe in the same god : the act of worshipping God or a god

Praise - to say or write good things about (someone or something) : to express approval of (someone or something): to express thanks to or love and respect for (God)

Pray - to speak to God especially in order to give thanks or to ask for something

Bless - to ask God to care for and protect (someone or something): to provide (a person, place, etc.) with something good or desirable

Holy - exalted or worthy of complete devotion as one perfect in goodness and righteousness

Sin - an offense against religious or moral law

Repent - to feel or show that you are sorry for something bad or wrong that you did and that you want to do what is right

Salvation - the act of saving someone from sin or evil: the state of being saved from sin or evil

Purity - lack of guilt or evil thoughts

Yoke - a bar or frame that is attached to the heads or necks of two work animals (such as oxen) so that they can pull a plow or heavy load

Expectation - a belief that something will happen or is likely to happen : a feeling or belief about how successful, good, etc., someone or something will be

Plan - a set of actions that have been thought of as a way to do or achieve something

Goal - something that you are trying to do or achieve

Focus - a subject that is being discussed or studied: the subject on which people's attention is focused

Work - activity in which one exerts strength or faculties to do or perform something:

Manage - to take care of and make decisions about (someone's time, money, etc.

Experience - practical knowledge, skill, or practice derived from direct observation of or participation in events or in a particular activity

Leadership - the power or ability to lead other people

Vision - a thought, concept, or object formed by the imagination

Confidence - a feeling or belief that you can do something well or succeed at something

Communication - the act or process of using words, sounds, signs, or behaviors to express or exchange information or to express your ideas, thoughts, feelings, etc., to someone else

Yes - used to give a positive answer or reply to a question, request, or offer

No - used to give a negative answer or reply to a question, request, or offer

Start - to begin doing something

Stop - to not do something that you have been doing before: to not continue doing something

Money - something (such as coins or bills) used as a way to pay for goods and services and to pay people for their work

Invest - to commit (money) in order to earn a financial return

Debt - an amount of money that you owe to a person, bank, company, etc.

Surprise - an unexpected event, piece of information, etc.

Laugh - to show that you are happy or that you think something is funny by smiling and making a sound from your throat

Curiosity - the desire to learn or know more about something or someone

Fun - an enjoyable or amusing time

Memory - something that is remembered

Rest - freedom from activity or labor

Season - a time characterized by a particular circumstance or feature

Promise a statement telling someone that you will definitely do something or that something will definitely happen in the future

Finish - to reach the end of (something): to stop doing (something) because it is completed

Acknowledgements

How do you thank all the people who have poured out their lives into yours? My bride has been my constant companion and encourager! I could not do this without her. I must also thank Rick Bellerjeau, Adam Biesecker, Eric Helms and Rick Stepat. These four men have been great friends and encouragers who also hold me accountable and share their wisdom and thoughts.

Preface

It has been my desire to be very intentional about writing this book. You are probably asking yourself, who is this guy and how does he know what the 100 most important words are? There a millions of words, so how can he narrow them down to just 100?

These are the 100 most important words in my life. These are the words that have been a constant and true guide for me as I have walked this earth.

These are the words that I have taught my four children and hopefully one day will teach to my grandchildren as well.

This is not a profound statement, but I will say it anyway - words mean things! I have found that I must be very circumspect with the words that I use and more importantly, when I choose to use them.

Choose carefully the words you use throughout your life.

> *"Watch your thoughts, they become your words*
> *Watch your words, they become your actions*
> *Watch your actions, they become your habits*
> *Watch your habits, they become your character*
> *Watch your character, it becomes your destiny."*
> *- Anonymous*

Introduction

According to the Global Language Monitor, as of January 2014, there are over 1,025,000 words in the English language. So this book is only going to focus on 0.0001% of those words. Even though it is only 100 words, I truly believe they can have an incredible impact on you and your loved ones.

My goal is to encourage you to think about the words you use each day and to be very intentional about how you use them.

Hawk Nelson has written an incredible song called "Words". It is my son Jonathan's favorite song and I personally think it does a fantastic job of describing the impact that words can have on a person's life and more importantly - the impact of the words that we use. Read the lyrics and then really think about the song. I encourage you to buy the song and keep it your mobile device and listen to it often. It is a great lesson.

I have not really ordered the words in this book in terms of importance. I also have not listed them alphabetically. I only wanted to order the first word - Intentional and the last word - Finish. Other than that, I knew the list of words that I wanted to use, but put them in an order that seemed to flow for me as an author.

I hope you enjoy the book and that it can have a positive impact on your life.

The 100 Most Important Words

To Guide Your Life and Teach Your Children

Intentional

"The choice we face (in life) is between empty self-indulgence and meaningful activity". **Billy Graham**

<u>Definition: Intentional</u> - done in a way that is planned or intended

I wanted to start with the word Intentional. This word has meant so much to me over the past 10 years of my life. It drives the decisions that I make about my time, my talents and my treasure. I tend to be an A++ hyper personality. This means I have a lot going on all the time. If I am not careful, I can lose focus on the most important things in my life if I am not intentional about how I spend my time.

What are those important things in my life: Faith, Family, Friends and Fitness. So how am I Intentional in these key areas of my life?

With my faith, it is about having a set time for prayer, worship, study and fellowship. We are in church on Sunday, and back again on Wednesday. I get up in the morning to study and pray.

With my family it is about carving out time each week to focus on different individuals. I have a date night with my Bride, with four children it is very difficult to get that one on one time, so I have set up a weekly routine where Thursday evenings are dedicated to "daddy dates" with my girls and "boys bonding" with my sons.

With our friends, we have been very intentional about inviting both new and old friends over to the house for food and fellowship each month. We are intentional about inviting younger couples whom we can mentor, peers who we can share with and mature couples we can learn from.

With fitness, I have a morning routine of working out with goals and objectives to achieve.

Most importantly, we have been intentional about what we teach our children and the lessons we want them to learn. Parenting is not an adventure for the faint hearted or unprepared.

My challenge to you is as follows:

Consider how you can be more intentional this week in the following areas of your life:

Time - we all have the same amount of time each day (24 hours). How are you going to spend that time? Use a calendar and become very intentional about how you will use your time each day.

Talents - what are the skills and abilities that you have? Are you using them appropriately? How can you be more intentional about using your talents in a positive and meaningful way?

Treasure - this is a tough one for many people. Being intentional about how you spend, save and invest your money will take time and thoughtful effort on your part. If you are not good at this, then I would suggest someone like Dave Ramsey to help (www.daveramsey.com). You must know how each dollar is spent and how you are going to use your money.

If you can consistently be intentional about these three areas of your life, I believe you will find your life much more fulfilling.

Take the opportunity to be more intentional in your life

Finally, you will see as a recurring theme in the book, my reference to how you use your Time, Talents and Treasure. I believe that these are such key areas of your life that you need to consider how you use them wisely. I would also advocate that you must be intentional in every aspect of your life as well: Spiritual, Physical, Emotional, Financial, and Relational.

Homework - take the time this week to look at your calendar and determine how you can be more intentional with your time. If you can better control this one aspect of your life, then you can move on to other areas of your life.

Wisdom

"The only true wisdom is in knowing you know nothing." **Socrates**

<u>Definition: Wisdom</u> - the natural ability to understand things that most other people cannot understand

The older I get, the more important I realize it is to gain wisdom. There is not a single decision in my life where having more wisdom would not be a good thing.

Wisdom is very different than knowledge! Knowledge is something that you gain from books and learning. You can read an encyclopedia and gain knowledge on just about anything (or Wikipedia - but be careful with that source of that information).

From a biblical perspective, wisdom comes from God according to James 1:5. God certainly gave Solomon wisdom and he was known throughout all time as the wisest man.

A friend of mine recently asked me if he could pray for anything for me and my reply was - Wisdom, Wisdom, Wisdom.

It is often said that you can never have enough money. However, I would counter that you can never have enough wisdom.!

Wisdom is knowing about when to speak and when to be silent.
Wisdom is knowing when to praise and when to criticize
Wisdom is knowing when to act and when to reflect.
Wisdom is knowing when to say yes or when to say no.

As part of my daily routine, I read a chapter of Proverbs (there are 31 proverbs so this works out really well for a daily devotion).   It is always amazing to me that the proverbs seem fresh and real no matter how much I read them. I have been reading the proverbs for many, many years, and I am still find them incredibly useful.

Many of my favorite verses in the bible come from the book of proverbs. My pursuit of wisdom is a daily occurrence and until the day I die, I will be seeking wisdom.

<u>Homework</u> - start by reading proverbs. Seek out some of the wise people you know and spend time with them and be intentional about your conversations and the things you want to learn

Proverbs 4:5-8
Acquire wisdom! Acquire understanding!
Do not forget nor turn away from the words of my mouth.
"Do not forsake her, and she will guard you;
Love her, and she will watch over you.
"The beginning of wisdom is: Acquire wisdom;
And with all your acquiring, get understanding.
"Prize her, and she will exalt you;
She will honor you if you embrace her.

James 1:5
But if any of you lacks wisdom, let him ask of God, who gives to all generously and without reproach, and it will be given to him.

Character

"It was character that got us out of bed, commitment that moved us into action, and discipline that enabled us to follow through".
Zig Ziglar

Definition: Character - the way someone thinks, feels, and behaves : someone's personality

Character is something that we are constantly building into our children and something we "harp on" all the time. Character is really the embodiment of some many different qualities: Integrity, honesty, truthfulness, respectful etc. etc.

You will see many of these words throughout this book and they all roll up into what everyone would define as character.

We know good character when we see it and we know bad character when we see it as well.

When my children were younger we took them to the zoo one day and observed a family of four in front of us. It was a father, mother, teenage boy and a younger sister. They were in front of us in the line to pay for tickets. This is the conversation that we observed:

Father to Attendant: "We need four tickets - two adult and two children"

Son: "But Dad, I'm 14 and it says..."

Father: "Be quiet!"

Son: "But dad you have to be 12 or under to ...."

Father: "HUSH!"

Father to Attendant: "We need four tickets - two adult and two children"

Wow! I could not believe the lessons this father had just taught his children. He had just taught them that it was ok to lie (and I would say sell your integrity), to save $5.00.

I just cannot even begin to imagine the type of character that would be built into those children and especially that son. Since my children had witnessed this entire event, we took the time to sit them down and go over the entire event and explain what was wrong and how we did things in our family.

On another occasion, I had the opportunity to finish the basement of my house so my oldest son could have a room for himself. As we were about to begin construction, I asked many of my friends and neighbors (many of whom were professed Christians) about their experience and how best to proceed. To the person, they all told me NOT to apply for a building permit (even though that was the law) and to just get the work done quickly and nobody would know.

The reason they all gave me for not getting the building permit was as follows:

- It would take additional time.
- The permit would cost money.
- I would have to have everything inspected.
- My taxes would increase.

Needless to say, I did not heed their "advice". And you know what, they were right about every one of those things they called out. It took more time, it cost money and my taxes increased. But at the end of the day, I could look in the mirror and know I had done the right thing and tell my children (who watched then entire process and have me explain it to them) that our integrity and character was not for sale!

Our children are constantly watching us and want to know if we are going to do the right thing or not!

I have found that many of the instances of lack of character that I see revolve around money is some shape, form or fashion.

How will you build your character this week?   Who are you when nobody is looking?   Who are you when your children are watching you?

Know this, you are building character takes time – will it be good character or bad character? The choice is yours!

<u>Homework</u> - Choose this day to be a person of integrity in all your dealings (even with the IRS).   Consider the verse below and how God would look at your heart.

<u>1 Samuel 16:7</u>

But the Lord said to Samuel, "Do not look at his appearance or at the height of his stature, because I have rejected him; for God sees not as man sees, for man looks at the outward appearance, but the Lord looks at the heart."

Faith

"*Faith is taking the first step even when you don't see the whole staircase.*" **Martin Luther King, Jr**.

<u>Definition: Faith</u> -strong belief or trust in someone or something
: belief in the existence of God : strong religious feelings or beliefs

These next four chapters are a bit of a mantra in my life. When I am asked about what is most important in my life, I have a standard and quick reply - FAITH, FAMILY, FRIENDS, and FITNESS.

In our family it is our faith that defines who we are, what we do, and how we interact with others around us.

We all have faith! When you sit down in a chair you have faith that the legs will hold you up and not break. When you fly in an airplane, you cannot see the air but you have faith that aerodynamics will work and the plane will fly. Most of us have this kind of faith because it is something we can see, feel, touch or have demonstrated to us.

How do you explain faith in God? For me it is quite simple. I know what my life was like before God came into my life through his Son Jesus Christ and I know what my life is like now. I have seen prayers answered and the only explanation is God! I know that sounds simple, but it is childlike faith that God wants us to have!

I honestly do not know how anybody gets through this life without faith in God and the hope for the future. Faith is a very personal and intimate thing! It is something only you can experience for yourself.

It is my desire through this book to point others towards God using these 100 most important words.

<u>Homework</u> - Start today by reading the bible.   Start with the New Testament and read through Matthew, Mark, Luke & John and then Romans and Hebrews.   In the Old Testament read Proverbs and Psalms. Pray and ask God for his wisdom and discernment to understand the bible and to know Him on a more personal level. See key verses below.

Romans 10:17
So faith comes from hearing, and hearing by the word of Christ.

Ephesians 2:8
For by grace you have been saved through faith; and that not of yourselves, it is the gift of God;

Hebrews 11:6
And without faith it is impossible to please Him, for he who comes to God must believe that He is and that He is a rewarder of those who seek Him.

Family

"As the family goes, so goes the nation and so goes the whole world in which we live". **Pope John Paul II**

<u>Definition: Family</u> -a group of people who are related to each other

After faith, my family is the next most important priority in my life. My Bride and my four children are so incredibly important to me and I love them dearly.

This is a rather easy chapter to explain as to why family would be one of my top 100 words. We teach our children the importance of family and sticking together through thick and thin. We tell them that friends may come and go, but family will always be here for them.

There is a silly saying - " you can pick your friends, and you can pick your nose, but you cannot pick your family". That is true in the sense that you are born into a family and you had no choice in the matter. On the other hand, you absolutely have the choice of making family important in your life.

I know many of you have dysfunctional families or came from backgrounds where you did not have good examples for mothers and fathers. I understand and I can both sympathize and empathize. My parents divorced when I was young (as did my Bride's) and I had a very estranged relationship with my parents and siblings as a result of our dysfunctional family.

However, my Bride and I choose not to look into the past and let that define how our family of the future will be determined. We choose to carve a different pattern for our family and break any barriers of the past. In our future, family is and always will be important and we will be there for our children and our grandchildren no matter what!

Homework - If you came from a great family, call you family members today and tell them how grateful you are for them! However, just because you came from a bad home life does not mean that has to be your future. Start today to have a positive family future and become the family you always wanted.

Joshua 24:15

*If it is disagreeable in your sight to serve the Lord, choose for yourselves today whom you will serve: whether the gods which your fathers served which were beyond the River, or the gods of the Amorites in whose land you are living; but as for **me and my house**, we will serve the Lord."*

Friends

"Wishing to be friends is quick work, but friendship is a slow ripening fruit." **Aristotle**

<u>Definition: Friends</u> -a person who you like and enjoy being with

As I stated in the last chapter, we have the ability to choose our friends. We have the freedom of association in the United States and that is a blessing indeed.

I have heard it said that if you leave this life with five true friends, then you have had a great life.   I know that Facebook makes many people seem like they have hundreds and thousands of friends, but the reality is that we all only have a few real, true friends.

It is 3am and tragedy has struck your family.   Which friends would you call? I can only think of a couple of guys in my life I would immediately call and know they would be there for me (and I for them).   Those are the friends I am talking about.

Take the time to work and develop more meaningful relationships with these few friends.   You can always have a ton of acquaintances, but I would advise that you only have a handful of real friends with whom you can walk through this life together.

Friendship is never an easy thing, but the benefits are wonderful and fulfilling.   I am very grateful for the handful of true friends that I have.

Finally, I love the verses at the end of this chapter from Proverbs that describe friendship.   I encourage you to not just read them, but mediate upon them and see the wisdom in these words.

<u>Homework -</u> Call you best friends today and encourage them.   Set aside some time to get together and fellowship.

Proverbs 27:10

Do not forsake your own friend or your father's friend,
And do not go to your brother's house in the day of your calamity;
better is a neighbor who is near than a brother far away.

Proverbs 18:24

A man of too many friends comes to ruin,
But there is a friend who sticks closer than a brother.

Proverbs 17:17

A friend loves at all times,
And a brother is born for adversity.

Fitness

"If we could give every individual the right amount of nourishment and exercise, not too little and not too much, we would have found the safest way to health." **Hippocrates**

<u>Definition: Fitness</u> -the quality or state of being fit

This will be a very short chapter! I love exercise and running. I always have. I know that there is no persuasion in the world that will convince you to being fit and working out if you loathe the activity.

I will only say, that I am now 50 years old and run and exercise 6 days per week and I want to do everything in my power to be around for my children and grandchildren. Even though I am 50, I have an 11 year old son who is only going to get more active (just like his 21 year old brother). I owe it to my Bride and my children to take care of my body.

<u>Homework</u> - Start an exercise program today! Obviously check with your doctor first if you have not exercised in a long time.

<u>1 Corinthians 6:-20</u>
Or do you not know that your body is a temple of the Holy Spirit who is in you, whom you have from God, and that you are not your own? For you have been bought with a price: therefore glorify God in your body.

Hope

"Everything that is done in the world is done by hope." **Martin Luther**

<u>Definition: Hope</u> -to want something to happen or be true and think that it could happen or be true

We use the word hope quite a bit in everyday conversation and thought.

I <u>hope</u> he returns my phone call.   I <u>hope</u> she says yes.   I <u>hope</u> it does not rain.   I <u>hope</u> my team wins.   I <u>hope</u> the food at this restaurant is good.

The greatest hope we have for mankind is Jesus Christ.   It is only with changed hearts and renewed minds that our hope for the future can be better than our present situation.

I think the hymn - *My Hope is Built on Nothing Less* - by Edward Mote does an excellent job of explaining where our hope comes from.

My hope is built on nothing less
Than Jesus' blood and righteousness.
I dare not trust the sweetest frame,
But wholly trust in Jesus' Name.

Refrain

On Christ the solid Rock I stand,
All other ground is sinking sand;
All other ground is sinking sand.

When darkness seems to hide His face,
I rest on His unchanging grace.

In every high and stormy gale,
My anchor holds within the veil.

Refrain

His oath, His covenant, His blood,
Support me in the whelming flood.
When all around my soul gives way,
He then is all my Hope and Stay.

Refrain

When He shall come with trumpet sound,
Oh may I then in Him be found.
Dressed in His righteousness alone,
Faultless to stand before the throne.

Refrain

Where is your hope?   As for me, my hope is in God and his son Christ Jesus.   He is my firm foundation.

Homework - determine today where your hope lays.   What are you trusting in if not God?

Psalm 39:7
"And now, Lord, for what do I wait? My hope is in You.

Romans 5:3-5
And not only this, but we also exult in our tribulations, knowing that tribulation brings about perseverance; and perseverance, proven character; and proven character, hope; and hope does not disappoint, because the love of God has been poured out within our hearts through the Holy Spirit who was given to us.

Love

"Where there is love there is life." **Mahatma Gandhi**

"Tis better to have loved and lost than never to have loved at all."
Alfred Lord Tennyson

<u>Definition - Love</u> - a feeling of strong or constant affection for a person

The English language does a very inadequate job of describing the word love. We have to use inflection, tone of voice and context to convey the type of love we are talking about. The Ancient Greeks had a much better way of expressing love with different words:

Agape - means love in a "spiritual" sense.

Eros - is "physical" passionate love, with sensual desire and longing. Romantic, pure emotion without the balance of logic.

Philia - is "mental" love. It means affectionate regard or friendship in both ancient and Modern Greek. This type of love has give and take.

I have an Agape Love for God and my fellow brothers and sisters in Christ.

I have an Eros Love for my Bride

I have a Philia Love for my friends and neighbors.

My life is incomplete without all three types of love evident in my life. I know that I am a better man for having loved my God, loved my Bride and loved my friends and neighbors. What a sad and wasted existence it would be in this world without love.

Homework - Where is the love of your life? What do you love most? Take the time today to show all three forms of love to those around you.

1 Corinthians 13:12-13

For now we see in a mirror dimly, but then face to face; now I know in part, but then I will know fully just as I also have been fully known. But now faith, hope, love, abide these three; but the greatest of these is love

Matthew 22:36-40

"Teacher, which is the great commandment in the Law?" And He said to him, "'You shall love the Lord your God with all your heart, and with all your soul, and with all your mind.' This is the great and foremost commandment. The second is like it, 'You shall love your neighbor as yourself.' On these two commandments depend the whole Law and the Prophets."

Joy

"Joy is a net of love by which you can catch souls." **Mother Teresa**

<u>Definition - Joy</u> - a feeling of great happiness

The opposite of joy is sadness. I do not know anybody who would make the conscious decision to be sad rather than joyful and yet how many people do we know who walk around with a sad look on their face.

You can choose to be joyful and bring joy into others' lives. Joy has nothing to do with our situation as much as it has to do with our attitude and outlook on life.

I have heard it said that pure joy comes from serving others. I truly believe this. There is nothing more selfless than a volunteer helping others and bringing joy (and perhaps peace) into their lives.   We take the focus off of ourselves and shine the light on others.   In this setting, our situation and circumstances diminish as we focus on serving others and meeting their needs.

Think about the most joyful times in your life.   They were probably when you were serving others, or perhaps when others were serving you!!

<u>Homework</u> - take the opportunity to think about people you can serve and be intentional about bringing joy into their lives.

Psalm 98:4-5
Shout joyfully to the Lord, all the earth;
Break forth and sing for joy and sing praises.
 Sing praises to the Lord with the lyre,
With the lyre and the sound of melody.

Proverbs 15:13

A joyful heart makes a cheerful face, But when the heart is sad, the spirit is broken.

3 John 1:4

I have no greater joy than this, to hear of my children walking in the truth.

Peace

"A people free to choose will always choose peace." **Ronald Reagan**

<u>Definition - Peace</u> - a state in which there is no war or fighting

Peace and tranquility.   That is what I look forward to when I come home from a hectic day of work and a long commute.   My Bride does an excellent job of knowing that our home is a refuge and a place to bring peace and tranquility.

We are by no means perfect.   There is certainly conflict and fights (we are after all a family of six people with strong opinions).   However, peace is the norm and conflict is the exception to the rule.   We teach our children about being peaceful and creating an atmosphere of peace and tranquility. It is easier said than done, but we intentionally make an effort to have a peaceful home.

Are you a peacemaker or do you enjoy conflict?   Blessed are the peacemakers, for they shall be called the Sons of God. Matthew 5:9.

<u>Homework</u> - is there anybody that you need to make peace with today? Do not hesitate.   Seek them out and make the peace.

2 Thessalonians 3:16
Now may the Lord of peace Himself continually grant you peace in every circumstance. The Lord be with you all!

Isaiah 9:6

For a child will be born to us, a son will be given to us; And the government will rest on His shoulders; And His name will be called Wonderful Counselor, Mighty God, Eternal Father, Prince of Peace.

Patient/Patience

"He that can have patience can have what he will." **Benjamin Franklin**

<u>Definition - Patient</u> - able to remain calm and not become annoyed when waiting for a long time or when dealing with problems or difficult people

I heard the story of the mother who needed more patience dealing with her children. She lifted up the following prayer:

"Lord, give me patience to deal with my children and give it to me now!"

A somewhat incongruent prayer, but I completely understand the sentiment. I want more patience and I want it now!!

I have also found that patience leads to much better decision making. In Proverbs, it teaches that one person's story sounds good concerning a conflict, but there are always two sides to every story. Patience would tell you to be slow to pass judgment until you have heard both sides of the story.

You must be patient when raising children. It is an 22 year marathon (my oldest is now 22) and I have realized as a parent that 22 years is still not long enough to get all the lessons in. I feel like I will be teaching my children lessons until the day I die.

Patience is not one of the fruits of the spirit by accident! Just like we do not give our children everything they ask for, when they ask for it. God wants to grow us and build us up.

What I have found in my life is that patience comes through the experiences, trials and tribulations that are placed in my path.

<u>Homework</u> - what are you currently impatient about? Is it really that critical?   I would encourage you to pray about it and seek wise council from others who have been down a similar path.

<u>Colossians 1:10-12</u>
so that you will walk in a manner worthy of the Lord, to please Him in all respects, bearing fruit in every good work and increasing in the knowledge of God; strengthened with all power, according to His glorious might, for the attaining of all steadfastness and patience; joyously giving thanks to the Father, who has qualified us to share in the inheritance of the saints in Light.

Kindness

"Kindness is the language which the deaf can hear and the blind can see." **Mark Twain**

<u>Definition - Kindness</u> - the quality or state of being kind

I have found that kindness is usually little things that people do for each other: Kindness usually does not cost much (from a tangible point of view), but pays huge dividends

Holding opening the door when someone's hands are full.

Paying the toll for the person behind you.

A handwritten note, text, tweet or Facebook post, or email at just the right time.

The kind word to a work associate who has had a tough day

Kindness is something that is "caught" and not "taught". You will need to demonstrate kindness in front of your children for them to really get the lesson.

<u>Homework</u> - look for opportunities to be kind this week to people you know and love as well as complete strangers.

<u>Proverbs 3:3</u>
Do not let kindness and truth leave you; Bind them around your neck, Write them on the tablet of your heart.

Goodness

"Man has two great spiritual needs. One is for forgiveness. The other is for goodness". **Billy Graham**

<u>Definition - Goodness</u>- the quality or state of being good

What is opposite of being good? Being bad! Do we ever have to tell your children how to be bad? NO! But we are constantly pushing them to be "good".   Goodness is a condition of the heart.   Being good is what leads (and should lead) to acts of kindness.

Goodness is closely tied with kindness that we just read about in the previous chapter.   Kindness and goodness are always inexorably linked.

Goodness is a character quality of God. Psalm 136:1 - Give thanks to the Lord for He is Good - his love endures forever.

Around our church you will hear people in conversation ask how they are doing and the response will be:

"God is good" to which the reply is - "All the time".

<u>Homework</u> - look for ways to improve the goodness in your life and then use acts of kindness as a tangible outpouring of your goodness

Psalm 23:5-6
You prepare a table before me in the presence of my enemies;
You have anointed my head with oil; My cup overflows.
Surely goodness and loving kindness will follow me all the days of my life, And I will dwell in the house of the Lord [d]forever.

Faithful (ness)

"God has been faithful time and again to surround me with people that sharpen me and that make me better". **TobyMac**

<u>Definition - Faithful</u>- having or showing true and constant support or loyalty
: deserving trust : keeping your promises or doing what you are supposed to do
: not having sex with someone who is not your wife, husband, girlfriend, or boyfriend

Did you read the definitions above?   Really read them?   Read them again!

Our world is sorely lacking in faithfulness!   The divorce rate is 50%, promises are not kept, and people cannot be trusted!   Faithfulness is most definitely an outward character quality that others can see.   People know if you are faithful or not!

What will your legacy of faithfulness be for your family?   Many of us did not have good examples from our parents or loved ones, but that is not an excuse for not being faithful!

I do not look to other people as example of faithfulness.   I look to God.   God has been so faithful in my life!   God constantly meets my needs and has never let me down.   He is a good "daddy".

On the next page is a great hymn that describes God's faithfulness.   I encourage you to go to the internet and listen to the song.   It is a magnificent testimony to Gods character.

Great is Thy Faithfulness

Refrain

Great is Thy faithfulness!
Great is Thy faithfulness!
Morning by morning new mercies I see.
All I have needed Thy hand hath provided;
Great is Thy faithfulness, Lord, unto me!

Great is Thy faithfulness, O God my Father;
There is no shadow of turning with Thee;
Thou changest not, Thy compassions, they fail not;
As Thou hast been, Thou forever will be.

Refrain

Summer and winter and springtime and harvest,
Sun, moon and stars in their courses above
Join with all nature in manifold witness
To Thy great faithfulness, mercy and love.

Refrain

Pardon for sin and a peace that endureth
Thine own dear presence to cheer and to guide;
Strength for today and bright hope for tomorrow,
Blessings all mine, with ten thousand beside!

Refrain

Homework - are you being faithful in all aspects of your life? Your time, talents and treasures? Your relationships? Take time this week to reflect of your life and how you can be more faithful in all these areas of your life.

Psalm 89:1

I will sing of the lovingkindness of the LORD forever;
To all generations I will make known Your faithfulness with my
mouth.

Psalm 36:5

Your loving kindness, O Lord, extends to the heavens, Your
faithfulness reaches to the skies.

Lamentations 3:22-24

The Lord's loving kindnesses indeed never cease,
For His compassions never fail.
They are new every morning;
Great is Your faithfulness.
"The Lord is my portion," says my soul,
"Therefore I have hope in Him."

Gentleness

"Gentleness is the antidote for cruelty." **Phaedrus**

<u>Definition - Gentleness</u> - the quality or state of being gentle; ESPECIALLY : mildness of manners or disposition

I often think of gentleness in terms of my speech and how I talk to others. More often than not, I use cruel words that can cut to the very marrow and harm a person for years.

Proverbs 15:1 is a good illustration of how gentle words can calm a difficult situation.

Proverbs 15:1

A gentle answer turns away wrath,
But a harsh word stirs up anger.

Many times I have found in conversations with my adult children that I have to count to 10 (very slowly) before I respond. A quick response from me during a difficult conversation is usually not kind, loving or gentle. Invariably, when I try the "gentle" approach, my words will break through even the toughest barriers.

I have found with my daughters and my Bride that gentleness is almost always a better approach than condemnation. It is a learned skill for me and not one that I grew up with. I know that for the rest of my life, I will need to seek God and his wisdom to make gentleness something that is evident in my life all the time and not just some of the time.

<u>Homework</u> - are you a gentle person? If not, what is your excuse? Seek God and ask him to bring gentleness into your life. See the verses on the next page as a starting point.

Psalm 18:35

You have also given me the shield of Your salvation, And Your right hand upholds me; And Your gentleness makes me great.

Ephesians 4:1-3

Therefore I, the prisoner of the Lord, implore you to walk in a manner worthy of the calling with which you have been called, with all humility and gentleness, with patience, showing tolerance for one another in love, being diligent to preserve the unity of the Spirit in the bond of peace.

1 Timothy 6:11

But flee from these things, you man of God, and pursue righteousness, godliness, faith, love, perseverance and gentleness.

Self-Control

"*Industry, thrift and self-control are not sought because they create wealth, but because they create character*". **Calvin Coolidge**

Definition - Self-Control - restraint exercised over one's own impulses, emotions, or desires

What areas of our life do we need self-control?

Diet?
Exercise?
Prayer?
Discipleship?
Study?
Work?
Internet Surfing?
Social Networking?
Spending?
Saving?
Thoughts?
Speech?
Actions?

Note that I have listed the following: - Physical, Spiritual, Emotional, Financial and Relational aspects of our lives. The point being that we need self-control in **EVERY** area of our life!!

I find that I can exercise self-control in some areas better than others. I am a fanatic when it comes to exercise, but eat like a slob!! I attend church every Sunday, but struggle in my personal devotions and prayer. I can save money very diligently, but then make a foolish purchase.

What kind of example will you be to your children and your Bride?   They will either see evidence of self-control in your life or lack thereof!   It is not enough to teach self-control - we must live it out every day in our life.

Homework - make a list of the areas of your life where you believe you exercise great self-control and the reason why you believe you have been successful.   Now make an additional list of those areas of your life where you do not have self-control and list the reasons that are holding you back from being in self-control.

Titus 1:7-9

For the overseer must be above reproach as God's steward, not self-willed, not quick-tempered, not addicted to wine, not pugnacious, not fond of sordid gain, but hospitable, loving what is good, sensible, just, devout, self-controlled, holding fast the faithful word which is in accordance with the teaching, so that he will be able both to exhort in sound doctrine and to refute those who contradict.

1 Corinthians 9:24-25

Do you not know that those who run in a race all run, but only one receives the prize? Run in such a way that you may win. 25 Everyone who competes in the games exercises self-control in all things. They then do it to receive a perishable wreath, but we an imperishable.

Mercy

"I have always found that mercy bears richer fruits than strict justice." **Abraham Lincoln**

<u>Definition - Mercy </u>- kind or forgiving treatment of someone who could be treated harshly

During the civil war (1861-1865) Gen. Joseph Hooker once sent an envelope to the president containing the cases of 55 convicted and doomed deserters; Lincoln merely wrote "Pardoned" on the envelope and returned it to Hooker.

Mercy is not getting what we deserve! President Lincoln was famous for offering mercy to many condemned men during the civil war. By the law, they deserved death! However, time and again he chose mercy instead.

When my bride and I were first married, we took a test that showed us our spiritual gifts. Each was measured on a scale of 0 to 30.   When it came to mercy, I scored a zero and my bride scored a 30. Quite a contrast. However, as we have lived more life and encountered more situations our scores have changed!   My score is now about 15 and my Brides score is about 20.   Sometimes I am more merciful than she is! The older I get, the more merciful I become.

Where would you score on the mercy test?

The greatest mercy in life is the mercy God shows us through his son Jesus. We are all sinners and deserving of death and hell, and yet he made a way for us to receive mercy through the shed blood of his son Jesus on the cross.   Mercy is deliverance from judgment.

We teach our children about God's mercy and grace in our lives and how Jesus bore our sins on the cross and delivered us death.

<u>Homework</u> - is there anybody that you need to show mercy to today? Take the time to seek them out and show them mercy. Of course they do not deserve it! It would not be mercy if they did.

Matthew 5:7

"Blessed are the merciful, for they shall receive mercy.

Titus 3:5

He saved us, not on the basis of deeds which we have done in righteousness, but according to His mercy, by the washing of regeneration and renewing by the Holy Spirit,

Ephesians 2:4-5

But God, being rich in mercy, because of His great love with which He loved us, even when we were dead in our transgressions, made us alive together with Christ (by grace you have been saved),

Grace

"Saving faith is an immediate relation to Christ, accepting, receiving, resting upon Him alone, for justification, sanctification, and eternal life by virtue of God's grace." **Charles Spurgeon**

<u>Definition - Grace </u> - unmerited divine assistance given humans for their regeneration or sanctification

In the previous chapter I talked about God's mercy. Mercy and Grace really go together.

Mercy - not getting what we deserve
Grace - is getting what we do not deserve

God's grace is his gift to humanity. I have seen it explained this way with the following acrostic:

God's
Riches
At
Christ's
Expense

John Newton wrote this incredible hymn in 1779 and today it is the most famous hymn known. It is my favorite hymn and one that I want sung at my funeral. Read the words and meditate on the message.

Amazing Grace, how sweet the sound,
That saved a wretch like me.
I once was lost but now am found,
Was blind, but now I see.

T'was Grace that taught my heart to fear.
And Grace, my fears relieved.
How precious did that Grace appear
The hour I first believed.

Through many dangers, toils and snares
I have already come;
'Tis Grace that brought me safe thus far
and Grace will lead me home.

The Lord has promised good to me.
His word my hope secures.
He will my shield and portion be,
As long as life endures.

Yea, when this flesh and heart shall fail,
And mortal life shall cease,
I shall possess within the veil,
A life of joy and peace.
When we've been here ten thousand years
Bright shining as the sun.
We've no less days to sing God's praise
Than when we've first begun.

Homework - study the verses below and mediate on God's Grace!

Ephesians 2:8-9
For by grace you have been saved through faith; and that not of
yourselves, it is the gift of God; not as a result of works, so that no
one may boast.

1 Corinthians 15:10

But by the grace of God I am what I am, and His grace toward me did not prove vain; but I labored even more than all of them, yet not I, but the grace of God with me.

Colossians 4:5-6

Conduct yourselves with wisdom toward outsiders, making the most of the opportunity. Let your speech always be with grace, as though seasoned with salt, so that you will know how you should respond to each person.

Courage

"Courage is being scared to death... and saddling up anyway."
John Wayne

<u>Definition - Courage</u> - the ability to do something that you know is difficult or dangerous

I love John Wayne and regret that this current generation has no idea who he is. The quote above is so appropriate for defining courage.

Courage is a character trait that you can talk about at length, but only in demonstration does it become evident. I can tell my children to be courageous, but hopefully they will see me doing something courageous that will help the lesson sink in.

I think about the man who spoke up at a meeting and had the courage to say what I was thinking and endure the criticism that followed.

My oldest daughter had the courage to jump off a 30 foot cliff into the ocean. It gave me the courage to follow!!

The great thing about courage is that it is contagious! Others will rise to occasion and start to act courageously.

Courage is not only knowing the right thing to do in the face of opposition, but doing the right thing! You can prepare to be courageous by knowing how you will act and react to circumstances. Be prepared for the attitude and actions you will demonstrate when the opportunity presents itself.

<u>Homework</u> - think about how you can be more courageous at work, home, school or church. Is there a situation where you need to show courage? Do it today.

Psalm 31:24
Be strong and let your heart take courage, All you who hope in the Lord.

Mark 15:43
Joseph of Arimathea came, a prominent member of the Council, who himself was waiting for the kingdom of God; and he gathered up courage and went in before Pilate, and asked for the body of Jesus.

Honor

"I would prefer even to fail with honor than win by cheating."
Sophocles

<u>Definition - Honor</u> - respect that is given to someone who is admired

Some people think honor is something that is turned on and off like a water spigot. Apparently they believe you can act honorably is some situations, but not others.

We have a friend of ours who is so competitive, that he will cheat at Sunday school church games (these are games with children), rather than lose. When he told me that I was floored! There is no honor in the victory and certainly no good lesson for the children to learn.

Honor is about respect and dignity! The first commandment with a promise is about honoring our father and mother. This means to respect them and the wisdom and knowledge that they have gained.

Honor is about doing the right thing, even when others within your peer group might disagree with you (and even call you crazy). I remember watching a documentary on the civil rights movement and it showed a KKK rally in some town. There were only a handful of KKK members marching down the street and they were attacked by an obviously agitated crowd. I remember one of the KKK members being knocked to the ground and beset upon by the crowd. Suddenly, a young African American lady came along and covered his body with her body and made the crowd stop. She protected him until the police could come and take him away. She acted honorably in a very terrible situation. Her peer group was obviously not happy with her, but she chose to protect instead of attack. There is no doubt she disagreed with the KKK behavior, she just chose not to resort to violence. She acted with honor.

The Medal of Honor is the highest award for valor in action against an enemy which can be given to an individual serving in the Armed Services of the United States. It is normally presented to its recipient by the President in the name of Congress. Honor is the key word in the award and everybody recognizes the significance of the award.

Make honor an integral part of who you are and what your family will believe and act upon.

<u>Homework</u> - read the stories valor and honor at http://www.cmohs.org/

Ephesians 6:2-3
Honor your father and mother (which is the first commandment with a promise), so that it may be well with you, and that you may live long on the earth.

Romans 12:10
Be devoted to one another in brotherly love; give preference to one another in honor;

Proverbs 15:33
The fear of the Lord is the instruction for wisdom, And before honor comes humility.

Integrity

"The supreme quality for leadership is unquestionably integrity. Without it, no real success is possible, no matter whether it is on a section gang, a football field, in an army, or in an office."
Dwight D. Eisenhower

"Integrity is doing the right thing, even when no one is watching."
C.S. Lewis

<u>Definition - Integrity</u> - the quality of being honest and fair

I love the C.S. Lewis quote on integrity. It is something I heard when I was a young man and it is stuck with me ever since.

I think about the stories you will occasionally hear in the news about someone who finds an incredible amount of money and does the right thing - by returning the money to its rightful owner. The finder of the money could have kept it and nobody would have known, but integrity of character compels them to do the right thing!

Do you do the right think when no one else is watching? I can promise you this - if you have children - they are always watching and learning. They will know in a New York minute if you are a person of integrity or not. Be watchful and mindful of you actions regarding integrity - especially when it comes to money and finances. I have seen too many people willing to sell their integrity to save a few dollars! Don't be that kind of person.

<u>Homework</u> - exam your life and determine if there are areas where you lack integrity.   Be honest with yourself and seek God's forgiveness and make integrity an integral part of your life.

Proverbs 10:9
He who walks in integrity walks securely, But he who perverts his ways will be found out.

Proverbs 20:7
A righteous man who walks in his integrity — How blessed are his sons after him.

Reputation

"It takes 20 years to build a reputation and five minutes to ruin it. If you think about that, you'll do things differently." **Warren Buffett**

<u>Definition - Reputation</u>: the common opinion that people have about someone or something: the way in which people think of someone or something

In the previous chapter on Integrity we saw that it is a character quality that is sometimes exemplified by who you are when no one else is watching.

A reputation, on the other hand is "earned" by your outward actions that others will see.   A good reputation can carry you far!   Just as a bad reputation can be an anchor that holds you down and holds you back.

When I was in school - if a girl had a "reputation" it meant that she was an easy sex target and willing "put out".   Once this designation was hung on her, it would be very difficult to shed. Her reputation will follow her for many years to come.

I think about Tim Tebow as a young man who has an incredible positive reputation and he works hard to maintain that positive reputation. He is careful and thoughtful about what he says, where he goes, who he is with and the actions he takes.   He knows that he is under a microscope all the time and many people are waiting for him to fail so that they can impugn his reputation.

What is your reputation in the following areas?

Work, School, Church, Family, Finances, Marriage, Relationships?

Homework - examine all areas of your life and determine whether or not you have a good reputation in all of them. If not, develop a plan to work on those areas that will lead to a good reputation in the future.

Acts 6:3

Therefore, brethren, select from among you seven men of good reputation, full of the Spirit and of wisdom, whom we may put in charge of this task.

Loyal/Loyalty

"Loyalty and friendship, which is to me the same, created all the wealth that I've ever thought I'd have." **Ernie Banks**

<u>**Definition - Loyal**</u> - having or showing complete and constant support for someone or something

People are very loyal to certain things - sports teams, pets, jobs, relationships etc.

In the South you find out about sports loyalties very quickly!

When I lived in Alabama it was all about - Alabama and Auburn.

When I lived in South Carolina it was all about - South Carolina and Clemson.

When I lived in Texas it was all about - Texas and Texas A&M.

When I lived in Georgia it was all about - Georgia and Georgia Tech.

How do you know people are loyal to their team? They cheer for them whether they win or lose. They wear the team colors and fly flags outside their homes. They have license plates on their cars and key chains with logos. It is usually not to difficult to know where someone's sports loyalties lie.

Loyalty is an admirable character quality to teach our children. However, I fear we are too quick to teach them about sports loyalties and not about those loyalties that really matter in life!

Loyalty to our marriage and our Bride! Loyalty to our job and boss! Loyalty to our friends and neighbors! Loyalty to our family!

I encourage you this day to choose to whom you will be loyal and make the effort so that others can see evidence of this loyalty in your life.

Homework - Where do your loyalties lie?   Take the time to examine what you are most loyal to in your life and determine if it the really important things our just "stuff".

Joshua 24:15
If it is disagreeable in your sight to serve the Lord, choose for yourselves today whom you will serve: whether the gods which your fathers served which were beyond the River, or the gods of the Amorites in whose land you are living; but as for me and my house, we will serve the Lord."

Proverbs 20:28
Loyalty and truth preserve the king, and he upholds his throne by righteousness.

Proverbs 21:21
He who pursues righteousness and loyalty finds life, righteousness and honor.

Hosea 6:6
For I delight in loyalty rather than sacrifice,
And in the knowledge of God rather than burnt offerings.

Forgive/Forgiveness

"We cannot embrace God's forgiveness if we are so busy clinging to past wounds and nursing old grudges." **T. D. Jakes**

<u>Definition - Forgive</u> - to stop feeling anger toward (someone who has done something wrong) : to stop blaming (someone) : to stop feeling anger about (something) : to forgive someone for (something wrong) : to stop requiring payment of (money that is owed)

Debbie and I could not have survived these 20+ years of marriage without forgiveness. It is just not possible. We see so many couples who are bitter and angry and never learn to forgive. They truly are the ones who are trapped by their un-forgiveness.

For me, the bible is the best source for guidance on forgiveness. The central theme of the Bible is Christ dying on the cross for our sins and all we have to do is ask forgiveness from our sins and God will forgive us because of what Christ did for us on the cross.

If you have not forgiven your spouse for something, then consider these verses and decide if you can still not forgive.

Should we forgive or not?

<u>**Matthew 6:14-15 – 14**</u> *For if you forgive others for their transgressions, your heavenly Father will also forgive you. 15 But if you do not forgive others, then your Father will not forgive your transgressions.*

<u>**Ephesians 4:32 – 32**</u> *Be kind to one another, tender-hearted, forgiving each other, just as God in Christ also has forgiven you.*

Colossians 3:13 – *bearing with one another, and forgiving each other, whoever has a complaint against anyone; just as the Lord forgave you, so also should you.*

How many times should we forgive?

Matthew 18:21-22 - 21 *Then Peter came and said to Him, "Lord, how often shall my brother sin against me and I forgive him? Up to seven times?" 22 Jesus *said to him, "I do not say to you, up to seven times, but up to seventy times seven.*

Finally – How true Love and Forgiveness go hand in hand

1 Corinthians 13-4:5 -4 *Love is patient, love is kind and is not jealous; love does not brag and is not arrogant, 5 does not act unbecomingly; it does not seek its own, is not provoked, does not take into account a wrong suffered,*

Love keeps no record of wrongs.

Finally, Matthew West has an incredible song called - Forgiveness. The song was inspired by the story of Renee Napier and her ability to forgive the man who killed her daughter Megan. Read the words to this song and think about how you would have reacted to this same situation. I honestly do not know if I would have the courage to forgive the way she did.

Visit their website to read this incredible story.

www.themeagannapierfoundation.com

Homework - is there someone you need to forgive? Do not let anger and hatred eat you alive. Pray that you would have the courage to forgive.

Psalm 86:5
For You, Lord, are good, and ready to forgive, And abundant in loving kindness to all who call upon You.

Thoughtful /Thoughtfulness

"Give back in some way. Always be thoughtful of others. "
Jackie Joyner-Kersee

<u>**Definition - Thoughtful**</u> - showing concern for the needs or feelings of other people

When I think of thoughtfulness, I think of my daughters, Sarah and Hannah. They are both so in tune with others feelings that they just seem to know how to be thoughtful as a natural part of their very being. I attribute this to my Bride!

My Bride is the most thoughtful person I know. She is always concerned with others needs and desires and is looking for ways to bless others. Whether it is a family who needs a meal because of sickness or that phone call or text that touches somebody at just the right time. I truly believe that my daughters have observed their mother over the years and have mirrored her actions.

I think of the time when Hannah was having a really bad day. Her sister Sarah knew she was having a bad day and decided to take matters into her own hands. Sarah was going to the mall with some friends, but instead of shopping for herself, she spent the time looking for something special for Hannah.

Sarah settled on something simple yet would speak directly to Hannah. She went to the candy store where you can buy candy by the ounce. Sarah then proceeded not to just buy candy, but she went through the RUNTS and bought only the bananas. It was very time consuming and she spent her own money.   When she gave it to Hannah, it brightened here day considerably.

Hannah knew that one of her sorority sisters would be having a bad day as the anniversary of her father's death was looming. Hannah planned an entire day with her friend and treated her to some very special events. Her friend was incredibly touched by Hannah's kind gesture.

To be thoughtful you have to be intentional! You have to care about people and you have to make a sacrifice of your time, talents or treasure.

Homework - Think of someone this week that you can bless with a thoughtful act.   It might be as simple as a handwritten note dropped in the mail.   Be intentional and do something this week!

Philippians 2:4

do not merely look out for your own personal interests, but also for the interests of others.

Discipline

"Discipline yourself, and others won't need to." **John Wooden**

Definition - Discipline - a way of behaving that shows a willingness to obey rules or orders

The best definition of discipline I have heard is as follows:

Discipline = delayed gratification.

What a great way to describe the word. This works in terms of a parent disciplining a child so that they learn to obey (delayed gratification). It also applies in the sense of an athlete who has the discipline to train many months for a race and then has the satisfaction of winning the race after all of that preparation (delayed gratification).

We teach our children about discipline with their money (saving -vs- spending). We teach our children discipline with our time (early to bed early to rise). We teach our children discipline with our bodies (eating and drinking healthy foods).

I find that it is lack of discipline that causes me and my family so many problems. It is very easy to talk about discipline in the many facets of my life, it is a very different proposition to apply discipline to those facets.

Homework - read the book of Proverbs! It has some incredible wisdom when it comes to discipline.

Proverbs :20

Listen to counsel and accept discipline, that you may be wise the rest of your days.

Proverbs 15:32

He who neglects discipline despises himself, but he who listens to reproof acquires understanding.

Proverbs 23:12

Apply your heart to discipline And your ears to words of knowledge.

Honesty

"Honesty is the best policy." **Benjamin Franklin**

Polonius:
This above all: to thine own self be true,
And it must follow, as the night the day,
Thou canst not then be false to any man.
Farewell, my blessing season this in thee!
Hamlet Act 1, scene 3, 78–82

<u>Definition - Honesty</u> - the quality of being fair and truthful : the quality of being honest

Lying is opposite of honesty. I know that is not a revelation to anybody, but I think it is very important to juxtapose the two. Either you are a liar, or you are honest.

It is always amazing to me the lengths politicians will go not to call their opponent a liar. They will use other euphemisms to describe a liar, because to call someone a liar is a very serious charge. On the other hand, it seems that society and the world in general is ok with lying "as long as it does not hurt anyone".

In a court of law, they ask the witness to tell the truth, the whole truth and nothing but the truth. In other words, they are asking the witness to be honest. The fate of the trial depends on honest testimony. Our whole judicial system would come crashing down if witnesses were not compelled to be honest (nobody want to go to jail for perjury).

In Proverbs 6, Solomon tells us that lying is an abomination to God. God is looking for us to be honest in all aspects of our life.

We have to model honesty for our children.   Honesty is not something that will come naturally to them.   They have to see it in action and know the value of honesty (as well as the consequences for lying).

Opportunities to be honest in front or your children:

At the local restaurant when the children's menu says 10 and under only and your child is 11.

At the store when you accidentally leave an extra item in your shopping cart and realize you did not pay for it.

When you are helping your child with their IRS tax forms and showing them how to report **all** their income.

I did not make these examples up by happenstance.   These were all real life examples where my children are looking to me for honesty and leadership.   Kids are really smart and intuitive and they know if you are honest or not.   Choose this day to be honest! As Benjamin Franklin said " Honesty is the best Policy"

Homework – take the time this week to examine your life and determine if there are any areas where you have not been honest.   Take the steps necessary to make honesty an integral part of your life and decision making.

Proverbs 6:16-
There are six things which the LORD hates,
Yes, seven which are an abomination to Him:
Haughty eyes, a lying tongue,
And hands that shed innocent blood,
A heart that devises wicked plans,
Feet that run rapidly to evil,
A false witness who utters lies,
And one who spreads strife among brothers.

Exodus 20:16
"You shall not bear false witness against your neighbor."

Generosity

"Real generosity is doing something nice for someone who will never find out." **Frank A. Clark**

<u>Definition - Generosity</u> - the quality of being kind, understanding, and not selfish

The only way I know how to combat my own selfishness, it to be generous! It really is the only antidote to my selfishness.

When most people think about generosity, they think in terms of money and giving. Certainly giving money is a very tangible thing to do and is almost always appreciated.

Remember that generosity is not about the amount given! It is about the attitude and the sacrifice with which it is given. A reluctant or petulant giver or one who is giving out of their surplus is not the type of generous person God is looking for.

Luke 21:1-4

And He looked up and saw the rich putting their gifts into the treasury. And He saw a poor widow putting in two small copper coins. And He said, "Truly I say to you, this poor widow put in more than all of them; for they all out of their surplus put into the offering; but she out of her poverty put in all that she had to live on."

I would also argue that we must also be generous with our time and talents. Time is one commodity that is most precious to everyone and we all have the same amount of time available every day!

Generosity is not only for others. We must demonstrate generosity with our family members as well. Are we giving our Bride and children the time they deserve? Too many times I have spoken with men who said they wished their father has spent more time with them.

Are you using your special talents in a generous way? What are your spiritual gifts? Are you using those in a generous way?

When you do give money is it with a generous heart or is it reluctant? Do you teach your children to give and to do so generously? Do they see you giving generously?

__Homework__ – look for opportunities this week to be generous with your time, talents and treasures. If you can, involve your children and Bride so they can see firsthand an example of generous giving.

Proverbs 11:25
The generous man will be prosperous, And he who waters will himself be watered.

Proverbs 22:9
He who is generous will be blessed, For he gives some of his food to the poor.

2 Corinthians 9:7
Each one must do just as he has purposed in his heart, not grudgingly or under compulsion, for God loves a cheerful giver.

Share/Sharing

"We are not cisterns made for hoarding, we are channels made for sharing." **Billy Graham**

<u>Definition - Share</u> - to let someone else have or use a part of (something that belongs to you)

With four children you can imagine that sharing with one another can become an issue very quickly, if not dealt with in a fair and consistent manner.

Sharing comes up quite a bit when it comes to food (especially dessert).

What we have done is instituted the following rule. Suppose it is a last piece of cake that is being considered for sharing. What we do is let the first child cut the cake any way they want (big, small, equally divided, etc.). We then let the second child choose which piece they want! You only have to do this once or twice and the lesson is quickly learned. The child doing the cutting will almost always divide it as equally as possible. It is a great lesson for young children but also a good reminder for all of us.

<u>Homework</u> – look for opportunities to intentionally share this week. Think about how you can share your time, talents and treasures!

Ephesians 4:28
He who steals must steal no longer; but rather he must labor, performing with his own hands what is good, so that he will have something to share with one who has need.

Humility

"Humility is not thinking less of yourself, it's thinking of yourself less." **C. S. Lewis**

<u>**Definition - Humility**</u> - the quality or state of not thinking you are better than other people

There are people in this world that you meet and they are incredibly humble. When you talk to them, they always turn the conversation back to you and inquire about you and what you have accomplished.   When you leave a conversation with them, you almost always feel better as a person and somehow lifted up just by having talked to them.

Examples of humility –

> Volunteering to clean the restrooms and take on the hardest tasks of a project (and never calling attention to that fact).

> Thanking your co-workers and others when you receive accolades for a well-run project and giving them a shout out.

> Acknowledging all of those who helped you when you become the class valedictorian.

> Giving generously of your time, talents and treasures, but never revealing that to others.

Humility is probably one of the toughest character traits to accomplish because we are "wired" for praise and recognition.   Children can and do learn humility at home.   They will either learn to brag about themselves or learn to serve others and become humble.

Consider that God humbled Himself and took on human flesh and bone to save the world for its sin. Christ could have called down legions of angels to save him from the Cross, but he chose to die for you and for me. To God be the Glory!

Homework – pray this week that God will help you to be more humble in your dealings with your family, friends and co-workers. Look for opportunities to serve others without recognition.

Proverbs 22:4
The reward of humility and the fear of the Lord Are riches, honor and life.

Psalm 25:9
He leads the humble in justice, And He teaches the humble His way.

Proverbs 11:2
When pride comes, then comes dishonor, But with the humble is wisdom

.

Proverbs 29:23
A man's pride will bring him low, But a humble spirit will obtain honor.

Matthew 23:12
Whoever exults himself shall be humbled; and whoever humbles himself shall be exalted.

1 Peter 5:5
You younger men, likewise, be subject to your elders; and all of you, clothe yourselves with humility toward one another, for God is opposed to the proud, but gives grace to the humble.

Gratitude

"Feeling gratitude and not expressing it is like wrapping a present and not giving it." **William Arthur Ward**

<u>Definition - Gratitude</u> - a feeling of appreciation or thanks

I can remember when my two oldest children were very young and we found these stories and songs by "Patch the Pirate". One of the songs just stuck in our heads and we would sing it all the time. It was called the Gratitude Attitude. It was a great song that not only spoke to my children's heart, but also spoke to me as well

There are two saying we have in regards to being grateful:

"You get what you get and you don't pitch a fit"

"Be thankful for what you have"

Gratitude really is about the attitude of our heart and mind. It is so easy for us to look at others and be jealous of what they have or to forget all the blessing we have in our life.

Things I should be grateful for, but usually forget to praise God:

Good health, and the ability to walk! When I had hurt my foot years ago and could not walk at all, I became very conscious very quickly the blessing of being able walk.

Grateful for my Bride and Children
Grateful for my job and employment
Grateful for friends and family
Grateful for food, clothing and shelter
Grateful for a good night's sleep

Grateful for God's unconditional love
Grateful for our church, Sunday school and preacher

Being ungrateful is easy! We usually do not have to work real hard at that. Do not allow yourself or your family to be ungrateful, choose today to change your heart and attitude.   Choose to catch the "Gratitude Attitude"

Homework – make a list of all the things you are grateful for and put it on your refrigerator, on your phone or computer so you can see it every day.

Colossians 2:6-8
Therefore as you have received Christ Jesus the Lord, so walk in Him, having been firmly rooted and now being built up in Him and established in your faith, just as you were instructed, and overflowing with gratitude.

Encouragement

"Encouragement is the oxygen of the soul." **George M. Adams**

<u>Definition - Encouragement</u> - something that makes someone more determined, hopeful, or confident

I have heard it said that we should speak words of encouragement to our spouse and children ten times more than we should criticize them. In other words, for every one criticism, we should have 10 things to encourage them about.

You can encourage others in several ways:

> You can speak words of encouragement.

> You can send a note, text or e-mail of encouragement.

> Just your presence alone at a special event can be encouragement.

I have found when I am discouraged, the best way to get out of that "funk" is to encourage someone.   Encouragement is a contagious thing that just seems to multiply and pays huge dividends.   When you are encouraged, you want to encourage others and so on…….

You can work on being an encourager every single day.   In the bible there was a character whose name was Joseph, but they called him Barnabas (which means Son of Encouragement). What a great name!

When we went on a mission's trip to Cape Verde (West Africa), one of the team members created Barnabas bags. These were bags filled with a special treat and bible verse for each team member and was given at the beginning of each day to encourage the team in the work they were doing. It was a small gesture that went a long way towards making the team members feel loved and appreciated (especially after 12 days).

Encouragement can and should be a thoughtful act you perform every day! There will always be someone for you to encourage (even if it is yourself)

<u>Homework</u> – be intentional this week about encouraging someone. Go out of your way especially to encourage a stranger or someone you do not know that well. You just might make their day.

1 Thessalonians 5:11
Therefore encourage one another and build up one another, just as you also are doing.

Romans 15:4-6
For whatever was written in earlier times was written for our instruction, so that through perseverance and the encouragement of the Scriptures we might have hope. Now may the God who gives perseverance and encouragement grant you to be of the same mind with one another according to Christ Jesus, so that with one accord you may with one voice glorify the God and Father of our Lord Jesus Christ

Hebrews 3:13
But encourage one another day after day, as long as it is still called "Today," so that none of you will be hardened by the deceitfulness of sin.

Content
/Contentment

"Contentment is the only real wealth" **Alfred Nobel**

<u>Definition - Content</u> - pleased and satisfied : not needing more

We as Americans are so spoiled! The poor in our county are richer than most of people in the world. Our poverty level for one person (about $11,500) would make that person richer than 82% of the world's population.

We are never content! We never have enough, we can never get enough and we are never satisfied.

Contentment is most definitely an attitude of the heart and mind. While we should work hard and provide for our family, how much more stuff do we need?

Model contentment to your family and especially your children. Teach them to be content with what they have and to be satisfied. Generosity towards others and giving is a good way to help with contentment and meeting other's needs. Humility and patience are also key characteristics that can help to keep you content.

<u>Homework</u> – if you are not content, ask yourself why and then take the necessary steps to bring contentment (and ultimately peace) into your life.

2 Corinthians 12:10

Therefore I am well content with weaknesses, with insults, with distresses, with persecutions, with difficulties, for Christ's sake; for when I am weak, then I am strong.

Philippians 4:11

Not that I speak from want, for I have learned to be content in whatever circumstances I am.

1 Timothy 6:8

If we have food and covering, with these we shall be content.
I wanted to start

Hebrews 13:5

Make sure that your character is free from the love of money, being content with what you have; for He Himself has said, "I will never desert you, nor will I ever forsake you,"

Perseverance

"Perseverance is the hard work you do after you get tired of doing the hard work you already did." **Newt Gingrich**

Definition - Perseverance - the quality that allows someone to continue trying to do something even though it is difficult

Who needs to persevere? Everybody

When is perseverance needed? You just never know when you will need to persevere, so you need to be prepared all the time.

Where is it needed? In all aspects of our life - Spiritual – Physical – Emotional – Relational -Financial -

Why do you need to persevere? To complete the tasks, goals and objectives set before us.

Perseverance is not just for some sub-set of people, it for everybody.   It should be a key characteristic that describes who you are.   Do you give up easily or will you stick with the task until it is done.   The rewards in life are for those who persevere!   Your spouse and your children need to know you will persevere, especially in the tough times.

Homework – is there an area of your life where you need to persevere? If you need help, seek a family member to come along side you and help you to persevere.

1 Timothy 6:11
But flee from these things, you man of God, and pursue righteousness, godliness, faith, love, perseverance and gentleness.

2 Peter 1:5-7

Now for this very reason also, applying all diligence, in your faith supply moral excellence, and in your moral excellence, knowledge, and in your knowledge, self-control, and in your self-control, perseverance, and in your perseverance, godliness, and in your godliness, brotherly kindness, and in your brotherly kindness, love.

Flexible/Flexibility

"Stay committed to your decisions, but stay flexible in your approach." **Tony Robbins**

<u>Definition - Flexible</u> -willing to change or to try different things

My daughter told me the other day that I needed to be more flexible. What she meant was that she disagreed with my plans and objectives concerning dating and courting and wanted me to change them. In this instance, my Bride and I decided not to be flexible, because in some areas of life, we have made up or mind and flexibility would actually be a detriment.

While this is a negative example of flexibility, I wanted to start with this because while flexibility is usually a very good character quality, you must also know the areas of your life where and when you will not be flexible.

We can be flexible when it comes to job schedule, team practice schedule, time of church service, type of car driven etc. These are not typically life or death decisions. They may cause inconvenience or be annoying, but they will not generally speaking change your life.

I do believe that flexibility is a great quality and characteristic to have in your life as long as it does not cross a moral or ethical boundary or does not compromise the Christian belief or faith.

Some Areas where I would suggest we **should not** be flexible:

Consider other gods
Consider other books to be holy
Consider other paths to salvation/heaven
Consider situation ethics or behaviors

This is not an inexhaustible list, but just a few examples of where we need to take a stand and not be flexible.

<u>Homework</u> – are you flexible where you need to be flexible and are you inflexible where you need to be inflexible?

Philippians 4:12-13

I know how to get along with humble means, and I also know how to live in prosperity; in any and every circumstance I have learned the secret of being filled and going hungry, both of having abundance and suffering need. I can do all things through Him who strengthens me.

Change

"To improve is to change; to be perfect is to change often."
Winston Churchill

"The Only Thing That Is Constant Is Change -" **Heraclitus**

"The more things change, the more they remain the same"
Jean-Baptiste Alphonse Karr

<u>Definition - Change</u> - to make (someone or something) different

Most everybody hates change, or at least they say they hate change. In reality change surrounds us each and every day.   See what Solomon had to say about change in the verses below:

<u>Ecclesiastes 3:1-8</u>
There is an appointed time for everything. And there is a time for every event under heaven —

A time to give birth and a time to die;
A time to plant and a time to uproot what is planted.
A time to kill and a time to heal;
A time to tear down and a time to build up.
A time to weep and a time to laugh;
A time to mourn and a time to dance.
A time to throw stones and a time to gather stones;
A time to embrace and a time to shun embracing.

A time to search and a time to give up as lost;
A time to keep and a time to throw away.
A time to tear apart and a time to sew together;
A time to be silent and a time to speak.
A time to love and a time to hate;
A time for war and a time for peace.

You see, change is constant and never ending. You should embrace the change in life and learn to "roll with the punches". If you are open to the change then you will lead a much more full life.

What should really bring you comfort though is the fact that God does not change! Be encouraged by the verses below.

Malachi 3:6
"For I, the Lord, do not change;"

Hebrews 13:8
Jesus Christ is the same yesterday and today and forever.

Isaiah 40:28
Do you not know? Have you not heard?
The Everlasting God, the Lord, the Creator of the ends of the earth
Does not become weary or tired.
His understanding is inscrutable.

2 Timothy 2:13
If we are faithless, He remains faithful, for He cannot deny Himself.

James 1:17
Every good thing given and every perfect gift is from above, coming down from the Father of lights, with whom there is no variation or shifting shadow.

Psalm 102:25-28

"Of old You founded the earth,
And the heavens are the work of Your hands.
"Even they will perish, but You endure;
And all of them will wear out like a garment;
Like clothing You will change them and they will be changed.
"But You are the same,
And Your years will not come to an end.
"The children of Your servants will continue,
And their descendants will be established before You."

__Homework__ – work this week to be more accepting of the change that will come your way and model a positive behavior to your spouse and children.

Learning

"Tell me and I forget. Teach me and I remember. Involve me and I learn." **Benjamin Franklin**

<u>**Definition - Learning**</u> - the activity or process of gaining knowledge or skill by studying, practicing, being taught, or experiencing something

Learning never ends.

Learning never ends.

Learning never ends.

I repeated that three times for emphasis! You have to believe that learning never ends. From the day you are born to the day you die, your learning should never end.

According to the Jenkins Group:

• One-third of high school graduates never read another book for the rest of their lives.

• 42 percent of college graduates never read another book after college.

• 80 percent of U.S. families did not buy or read a book last year.

To keep your mind nimble and not grow complacent you must strive to continue your learning. Whether that is reading books, attending seminars, getting a formal degree or additional degrees, or learning a new skill, hobby or task.

I would advocate that we must apply learning to all areas of our life. Consider the book, websites, articles or magazines you could read to increase your knowledge in all of these area:

Spiritual – Physical –Emotional – Relational -Financial

You should model learning for your spouse and for your children. Show them that you are willing to learn and are not afraid to admit you do not know something. You will lead a much richer life for having learned something new.

<u>Homework</u> – read a book or learn a new skill or hobby this month.

Proverbs 1:5
A wise man will hear and increase in learning, And a man of understanding will acquire wise counsel,

Proverbs 9:9
Give instruction to a wise man and he will be still wiser, Teach a righteous man and he will increase his learning.

Teachable

"What I believe is that all clear-minded people should remain two things throughout their lifetimes: Curious and teachable."
Roger Ebert

<u>Definition - Teachable</u> - able and willing to learn

The preceding chapter on learning is followed closely with being teachable.

Teachable simply means a willingness to learn. It can and should be modeled for your spouse and children. They need to know that you are not a "know it all" and can be taught new things. A teachable attitude and spirit is critical for being productive and efficient.

The best attitude that I can tell you to convey is the following: "I don't know what I don't know". If you can live that and believe that, then you are ready to be teachable.

The beauty of the internet is that we have sites like YouTube that can be a great forum for learning.

Thing I learned how to do on YouTube:

I learned how to replace a radiator
I learned how to replace an alternator
I learned how to replace brake pads
I learned how to replace a broken screen on an iPhone
I learned new skills for Microsoft Office

Being teachable is an attitude and then an action. Chose today to be teachable

<u>**Homework**</u> – have someone our know teach you something new this week or go to YouTube and learn something new.

Proverbs 15:22

Without consultation, plans are frustrated,
But with many counselors they succeed.

Psalm 143:10

Teach me to do Your will,
For You are my God;
Let Your good Spirit lead me on level ground.

Attitude
(Positive)

"Your attitude, not your aptitude, will determine your altitude."
Zig Ziglar

<u>Definition - Attitude</u> - the way you think and feel about someone or something

In this case I should have entitled the chapter "Positive Attitude". Nobody really cares for someone with a negative attitude. We would all rather be around someone with a positive attitude.

You may not always get to choose your circumstances or conditions, but you have 100% control of you attitude. If and when you realize this tidbit of wisdom, it can and will start to change your life.

You **<u>CAN</u>** choose to have a positive attitude today!

<u>Homework</u> – choose this week to have a positive attitude and model that for your Bride and Children.

<u>Philippians 2:14</u>
Do all things without grumbling or disputing; so that you will prove yourselves to be blameless and innocent, children of God above reproach in the midst of a crooked and perverse generation, among whom you appear as lights in the world,

<u>Colossians 3:23</u>
Whatever you do, work heartily, as for the Lord and not for men,

Motivation

"Motivation is what gets you started. Habit is what keeps you going." **Jim Ryun**

<u>**Definition - Motivation**</u> - the condition of being eager to act or work

Motivation can be tough some days! I know – some days I had no motivation to write this book On those days, I might only look up a word, or jot down a quick note or quote. They idea was to keep pushing forward and to keep moving.   Make progress and work toward the goal. I had to be flexible with my own self-imposed deadline (end of June and it is now July 7th).

What causes us not to be motivated.   Stress, fear, fatigue, hunger, lack of confidence?   These are all real disruptors of confidence and there are probably many others.   However, I would advocate that you should keep making small "baby steps" towards your goal and over time not only will you have made progress, but your motivation will return.

Also, having the right goal can help to keep you motivated! Consider Paul's goal

<u>Philippians 3:14</u>
I press on toward the goal for the prize of the upward call of God in Christ Jesus.

Paul was ship wrecked, beaten, tortured, thrown in jail, and had many other "bad" experiences.   Yet he knew his goal and what kept him going. If you have the right goals in life, they can be the motivation that keeps you going when the world is yelling to stop.

Consider motivational goals for all areas of your life: Spiritual – Physical – Emotional – Relational -Financial

Homework – motivation can be very contagious. Choose this week to be motivated to complete some long put off task, and bring your spouse and children along if possible.

Proverbs 14:23

In all labor there is profit,
But mere talk leads only to poverty.

Matthew 6:33

But seek first His kingdom and His righteousness, and all these things will be added to you.

Passion

"Light yourself on fire with passion and people will come from miles to watch you burn." **John Wesley**

<u>Definition - Passion</u> - a strong feeling of enthusiasm or excitement for something or about doing something

Passion without purpose or vision is wasted energy!

What are you passionate about? I am from the great state of Alabama and I can promise you that the people in that state are passionate about their football. There are only two teams in that universe – Alabama or Auburn (or better said –"Roll Tide" or "War Eagle").

I have seen people become passionate about the color of the carpet in the new church sanctuary (ready to come to blows if necessary).

I have seen people passionate about keeping a gasoline convenience store from being considered for a corner near their neighborhood. N IMBY

Most people do not lack passion! They lack focusing that passion on things that matter and are eternal.

What if husbands became passionate about their Brides? What would our marriage look like?

What if mothers and fathers became passionate about their children and their spiritual growth and needs? What would the next generation look like?

What if we as parents became passionate about serving God and leading our family in worship?

We do not lack in passion! We only lack in focus!!!

You can easily tell what people are passionate about. Just examine where they spend their time, talents and treasures and you will find out where their passions lie.

What are you really passionate about? Is it anything that really matters?

Choose today to be passionate about things that have eternal significance.

<u>Homework</u> – pull out your check book and your credit card statements for the last year and see where you are spending your money. Pull out your calendar for the past year and see where you spent your time. Can you do better in those areas of your life that really matter?

1 Corinthians 10:31
Whether, then, you eat or drink or whatever you do, do all to the glory of God.

Psalm 73:25-26
Whom have I in heaven but You?
And besides You, I desire nothing on earth.
My flesh and my heart may fail,
But God is the strength of my heart and my portion forever.

Responsible

"Most people do not really want freedom, because freedom involves responsibility, and most people are frightened of responsibility."
Sigmund Freud

<u>Definition - Responsible</u> - able to be trusted to do what is right or to do the things that are expected or required

Sigmund Freud is not usually someone who I am quick to quote, but in this instance, his quote above is spot on!!

My Bride and I often comment that when it comes to activities with our children, we are always going to be involved because we always want to know that a "responsible adult" will be on hand. We have seen too many times parents who want to be the buddy or friend, when what the children need is a responsible adult who can and will make wise and sometimes tough decisions.

Responsibility is something that is usually built up slowly over time. Think about a child earning a driver's license. In our state, it is a two year process involving a learners permit (and exam), a year of supervised driving, a provisional drivers license and then a full driver's license.

Why would they go to all this trouble? Many years ago you could just order your driver's license from the Sears& Roebuck catalog!! The reason for all the steps and time is because hard experience has shown that young people are not responsible drivers and need a long time to learn how to handle a car responsibly. Speeding down the road wrapped in 4,000 lbs. of steel is serious business.

Are you the responsible adult in the room? Do you step up to the plate and take responsibility? I hope you are and I hope you do!

- read the book of Proverbs! It has some incredible wisdom when it comes to responsibility.

Proverbs 22:6

Train up a child in the way he should go,
Even when he is old he will not depart from it.

Proverbs 6:6

Go to the ant, O sluggard,
Observe her ways and be wise,

Accountable

"We must reject the idea that every time a law's broken, society is guilty rather than the lawbreaker. It is time to restore the American precept that each individual is accountable for his actions."
Ronald Reagan

"You can expect, what you inspect" **W. Edwards Deming**

<u>Definition - Accountable</u> - required to be responsible for something

Each week on Thursday, my boss has everyone on the team submit their progress against their work projects. She reviews them over the weekend and at our staff meeting on Monday she goes through each one.

Not only does this keep all of us accountable, it also aids in conversation and alignment on priorities and allocation of resources.

Everyone is accountable to someone! Think of the military in terms of' accountability:

Private to Sergeant
Sergeant to Lieutenant
Lieutenant to Captain
Captain to Major
Major to Colonel
Colonel to General
General to Chief of Staff
Chief of Staff to Secretary of Defense
Secretary of Defense to President
President to God!

My oldest daughter and I were having a deep conversation regarding accountability and her desire not to be accountable to me on financial or scholarly matters (in other words - from her point of view -how she spent her money or the grades she made were none of my business).

We had a very long conversation that detailed the accountability that everyone has and that nobody is free to do what they please whenever if pleases them.

Accountability is a good thing to have in our lives whether it is financial, educational, relational, work, or spiritual. We all need someone who can ensure we are making wise and proper decisions on how to allocate the resources of our life (time, talents and treasures).

Homework - if you do not have accountability partners in your life, then starting today, seek out someone who can help hold you accountable in all they key aspects of your life.

"*Trust, but verify.*" **Ronald Reagan**

I use the Ronald Reagan quote about "Trust but Verify" all the time. Especially when dealing with strangers. They will often say - "don't you trust me" my response is "I trust, but verify"

Commitment

"The quality of a person's life is in direct proportion to their commitment to excellence, regardless of their chosen field of endeavor." **Vince Lombardi**

"There are only two options regarding commitment, you're either in or you're out. There's no such thing as life in between."
Anonymous

<u>Definition - Commitment </u>- a promise to do or give something

I love this fable on commitment involving a chicken and pig

> *A Pig and a Chicken are walking down the road.*
> *The Chicken says: "Hey Pig, I was thinking we should open a restaurant!"*
> *Pig replies: "Hm, maybe, what would we call it?"*
> *The Chicken responds: "How about 'ham-n-eggs'?"*
> *The Pig thinks for a moment and says: "No thanks. I'd be committed, but you'd only be involved!"*

The pig clearly understands that he would be "all in" and would have to sacrifice to make the business work. The chicken on the other had is only involved!

Which are you? Are you the chicken or the pig when it comes to being committed to your family, your job, your church your athletic team, your exercise, etc. etc. etc.

Commitment is not a sometimes thing, it is an always thing

Homework - determine if you are the chicken or the pig.

God's great commitment to Abraham!

Genesis 12:1-3

Now the LORD *said to Abram,*

"Go forth from your country,
And from your relatives
And from your father's house,
To the land which I will show you;
And I will make you a great nation,
And I will bless you,
And make your name great;
And so you shall be a blessing;
And I will bless those who bless you,
And the one who curses you I will curse.
And in you all the families of the earth will be blessed."

Respect

"He who wants a rose must respect the thorn." **Persian Proverb**

<u>Definition - Respect</u> - a feeling or understanding that someone or something is important, serious, etc., and should be treated in an appropriate way

In the military - Respect is expected and given to a higher ranking officer!

R-E-S-P-E-C-T   - Aretha Franklin asked for it!

I have heard it said that Respect is men's number one need in their life!

In the story below, the Pharisees were trying to trap Jesus, but Jesus turns their argument around on them and what is revealed is that Jesus was talking about respect!

<u>Mark 12: 13-17</u>

Then they sent some of the Pharisees and Herodians to Him in order to trap Him in a statement. They came and said to Him, "Teacher, we know that You are truthful and defer to no one; for You are not partial to any, but teach the way of God in truth. Is it lawful to pay a poll-tax to Caesar, or not? Shall we pay or shall we not pay?" But He, knowing their hypocrisy, said to them, "Why are you testing Me? Bring Me a denarius to look at." They brought one. And He said to them, "Whose likeness and inscription is this?" And they said to Him, "Caesar's." And Jesus said to them, "Render to Caesar the things that are Caesar's, and to God the things that are God's." And they were amazed at Him.

For the most part, respect is an "earned" character quality.   People will not respect you until you have earned that respect.   Trust is a heavy contributor to all aspects of respect.

I know that one of the worst things you can do is disrespect someone! Giving someone the proper respect can and will in most instances keep you from trouble and harm. When and individual feels disrespected, bad things usually follow.

Try being disrespectful to the following people and think about the consequences.

Police officer
Umpire/Game official
Judge
Doctor or Dentist
Nurse
Gate Agent at airport
Waiter or Waitress

Homework - are there areas of your life where you need to show respect? Reflect today and determine if you need to change your attitude towards someone who deserves your respect

Obedient

"The bottom line in the Christian life is obedience and most people don't even like the word." **Charles Stanley**

<u>Definition - Obedient</u> - willing to do what someone tells you to do or to follow a law, rule, etc. : willing to obey

Parable of Two Sons - Matthew 21:28-31

"But what do you think? A man had two sons, and he came to the first and said, 'Son, go work today in the vineyard.' And he answered, 'I will not'; but afterward he regretted it and went. The man came to the second and said the same thing; and he answered, 'I will, sir'; but he did not go. Which of the two did the will of his father?" They said, "The first."

Being obedient is central to the Christian walk and life. God did not give Moses the "10 suggestions". He gave him the 10 commandments. Jesus summarized the 10 commandments like this. Love God with all you heart and all your soul and all your mind and love your neighbor as yourself.

Being obedient to those two things is a full time job for all us. If we were to focus our obedience on that, then all of the other worries and cares of this world would fade away.

At home we have taught our children first time obedience. We do not count to 10, we do not count to 3. We give the command, hold up 1 finger and expect obedience from our children the first time without repeating ourselves. As benevolent parents, we always have our children's best interest in mind and they learn to trust that the obedience is good for them in the long run (that does not mean they will not test you or try you!).

<u>Homework</u> - practice you own obedience with God and his word before requiring your children or others to be obedient to your commands.

Ephesians 6:1
Children, obey your parents in the Lord, for this is right.

Colossians 3:20
Children, be obedient to your parents in all things, for this is well-pleasing to the Lord.

Sowing & Reaping

"Most of us spend the first six days of each week sowing wild oats; then we go to church on Sunday and pray for a crop failure." **Fred Allen**

<u>Definition - Sowing</u> - to plant seeds in an area of ground

<u>Definition - Reaping</u> - to get (something, such as a reward) as a result of something that you have done

I was out on a long run this morning as saw one of my neighbors working in his garden. It was early in the season and the plants were just starting to bloom. He had planted corn, squash, tomatoes, beans, peas and cabbage.

Do you think he would be surprised in the fall if his garden produced watermelons, cantaloupes, cucumbers and lettuce? That is just ridiculous right?

Of course he expects to see a bountiful harvest of exactly what he planted!

What are you planting (sowing) today? Are you sowing the fruits of the sprit - Love, Joy, Peace, Patience, Kindness, Goodness, Faithfulness, Gentleness, and self-control?

What do you think you will reap?

Why are we surprised when we sow the wrong seeds - (Hate, Anger, Disrespect, disobedience) and we expect a different harvest?

How foolish are we to think that our actions do not have consequences and that the law of reaping and sowing is not just as relevant today as it ever was in the past.

What are you sowing today?

<u>Homework</u> - Think about the positive things you have been sowing and consider the harvest you have been reaping. Try to be more thoughtful and circumspect this week with your actions and attitudes towards sowing and reaping.

<u>2 Corinthians 9:6</u>
Now this I say, he who sows sparingly will also reap sparingly, and he who sows bountifully will also reap bountifully.

<u>Galatians 6:7-8</u>
Do not be deceived, God is not mocked; for whatever a man sows, this he will also reap. For the one who sows to his own flesh will from the flesh reap corruption, but the one who sows to the Spirit will from the Spirit reap eternal life.

Choice(s)

"One's philosophy is not best expressed in words; it is expressed in the choices one makes... and the choices we make are ultimately our responsibility." **Eleanor Roosevelt**

<u>Definition - Choice</u> - the act of choosing: the act of picking or deciding between two or more possibilities

One of the more difficult things to teach your children about is choices and choosing.

We make hundreds of choices each day.

There are simple choices: When to get up, when to go to sleep, whether to exercise or not, what to eat or not eat etc. etc.

Then then are the more complex choices that do not come up every day, but can alter the very path we walk through life: Who do I choose to marry?   What job will I take?   Will I follow my parents teaching or reject them?

One of the more difficult things we have done as parents is allow our "adult" children to make choices that we know are wrong, and we can only sit back and watch the train wreck and help put the pieces together when the trauma has passed (the unfortunate reality is that sometimes there is nothing left to put together because a life ends)

Teach your children early to make good choices.   Model this behavior in front of them and explain to them why you made the choices you did.

I was just explaining to my daughter Hannah the other day, that when I am presented with a choice and someone is pressuring me to make a quick decision - my answer is almost always "no" or "wait". I have just found over time that if it is really a good opportunity or would have been good for me or my family, it will come back around again. If not, then I usually have not lost any ground (but there is of course the lost opportunity).

What big choices are you facing today? Here are some questions to ask and things to consider.

Are in in agreement and alignment with your spouse on these choices? Have you prayed about them? Have you sought wise counsel?

What are the potential consequences of these choices?

Homework - make a list of all the big choices you have to make in the next 6 months. Pray over your choices and seek wise counsel before making any big decisions.

1 Kings 18:21
Elijah came near to all the people and said, "How long will you hesitate between two opinions? If the Lord is God, follow Him; but if Baal, follow him." But the people did not answer him a word.

Joshua 24:15
If it is disagreeable in your sight to serve the Lord, choose for yourselves today whom you will serve: whether the gods which your fathers served which were beyond the River, or the gods of the Amorites in whose land you are living; but as for me and my house, we will serve the Lord."

Consequences

"Everybody, soon or late, sits down to a banquet of consequences."
Robert Louis Stevenson

<u>Definition - Consequences</u> - something that happens as a result of a particular action or set of conditions

In the previous chapter I talked about making choices. The net effect of any choice we make is that there will be consequences (either positive or negative).

My oldest son David (who was 21 at the time), came to us and told us he was dropping out of college and was going to pursue a career in music. Even though he is incredibly smart and was on the Dean's List.

Needless to say, we were not thrilled with this choice, so we sat him down and explained all of the consequences that would result from such a choice.

If he stayed in college, we would help him pursue his love of music, with funding for training and equipment as well as attendance and support for any concert he might have. He could continue to live at home rent free and enjoy all of the benefits of that (food, shelter, clothing etc).

However, if he chose to drop out of college he would have to move out and be responsible for 100% of his expenses and we would not support his music career in any shape, form or fashion

We explained that he would have much more time to pursue music if he was in college, because if he dropped out he would need to find a number of jobs to pay all of his living expenses.

I wish we could say he made the right decision, but he chose to drop out of college.   He is now working three part time jobs (janitor, barista, and customer service).   He has almost no time to practice his music and he has been living on friend's couches because he cannot afford a place to live.

He is basically homeless (by choice), and living out of his car.   It is tough to watch the train wreck, but we are convinced that the tough love we show him now and the negative consequences of his actions will bring him back home again and back to college or trade school and a real career.

The good news is that we continue to have very good and open communication with David and see him on a frequent basis.   He understands that we love him "no matter what", but that we disagree with the current path he has chosen to take.

Only time will tell if our tough love will prevail and our prodigal will return.   BTW – nobody told us that tough love was going to be tough on us!!!

Homework - Take some time to consider some of the good choices you have made and the consequences of those choices.   Write them down and celebrate them.   Then take some time to consider some of the poor choices you have made and the consequences of those choices.   Write them down and consider what you would have done differently and how you can help others to make good choices.

Colossians 3:25
For he who does wrong will receive the consequences of the wrong which he has done, and that without partiality.

Romans 6:23
For the wages of sin is death, but the free gift of God is eternal life in Christ Jesus our Lord.

Ephesians 6:1-3

Children, obey your parents in the Lord, for this is right. Honor your father and mother (which is the first commandment with a promise), so that it may be well with you, and that you may live long on the earth.

Disrespect - Disobedience - Dishonesty

"Ignoring a child's disrespect is the surest guarantee that it will continue." **Fred G. Gosman**

"Obedience is an act of faith; disobedience is the result of unbelief." **Edwin Louis Cole**

"Dishonesty is so grasping it would deceive God himself, were it possible. **"George Bancroft**

In our family, we call this the triple D.   These are the three things that will trip you up and get in in trouble so fast; it will make your head swim.

We will not tolerate disrespect, disobedience or dishonesty in our family. If you commit any of these three, then you will experience the fourth "D" and that is discipline.

Disrespect is one of those things that if you let it take hold in your house it will destroy it brick by brick.   At an early age, you have to teach your children to respect you and others as well.   Of course the tough part of this is - you must be worthy of respect!   You have to live your life in such a way that your children will want to respect you.

Disobedience must be dealt with swiftly and surely! The consequences for disobedience should be known and most importantly followed up on as stated. Our children know exactly what will happen if they are disobedient. They have seen us act quickly and with confidence when it comes to their brothers and sisters.

Dishonesty is probably the toughest of the three to model. Many people believe it is "ok" to tell a white lie (especially if money is involved). You have to really walk the talk and model this proper behavior in front of your children all time for them to know that "honesty is the best policy".

Homework - Take a hard look at your life and see if you are modeling the proper behavior. Are you disrespectful, disobedient or dishonest in any area of your life? Take steps today to be a positive role model.

Proverbs 6:16-

There are six things which the Lord hates,
Yes, seven which are an abomination to Him:
Haughty eyes, a lying tongue,
And hands that shed innocent blood,
A heart that devises wicked plans,
Feet that run rapidly to evil,
A false witness who utters lies,
And one who spreads strife among brothers.

Colossians 3:20
Children, be obedient to your parents in all things, for this is well-pleasing to the Lord.

H.A.L.T

Hungry - Angry - Lonely - Tired

"Fatigue makes cowards of us all." **Vince Lombardi**

I know that H.A.L.T is an acronym and not a word, but I wanted to include it in this book because this has been so important in my life and for my family.

Hungry
Angry
Lonely
Tired

I came upon this concept about 15 or so years ago and I wish I knew who to credit, but I cannot remember.

The premise of the acronym is that you should **HALT** any important decision making activity if you have any of these symptoms. The reason being is that you are apt to make a very poor decision if these symptoms are present.

What I have found is that the triggers for poor decision making are not all equal for me. I have found that hunger is a much bigger trigger for me than all of the others. However, more dangerous for me is to combine two or more of these symptoms.

If I am lonely and hungry, or tired and hungry, or angry and lonely, then I am in real danger of making a really bad decision. Things that would not tempt me or be an area of concern suddenly become quicksand and I easily be sucked in.

I have taught all of my children about HALT and it is quite humorous when they use it diagnose my mood and behavior.

One time I just "teed off" on my oldest son for no good reason and I was in the middle of a pretty good rant, when he calmly looked at me and said "Dad, have you had anything to eat lately?"   It was his way of respectfully saying - "hey dad, you are being a jerk right now so you might want to check yourself".   In this instance, he was absolutely right!   I was hungry. I got some food, took a deep breath and the situation calmed down.

You know yourself better than anybody, so be aware of the triggers in your life that lead to poor decision making and take precautions to keep them at bay.

Homework - Take the time to do a self-assessment and be truthful with yourself about the triggers in life that set you off.   Think about how you can better control these areas of your life and not let your guard down and allow temptation to bring you down.

Temptation

"Temptation is the devil looking through the keyhole. Yielding is opening the door and inviting him in." **Billy Sunday**

<u>Definition - Temptation</u> - something that causes a strong urge or desire to have or do something and especially something that is bad, wrong, or unwise

In the previous chapter I talked about H.A.L.T. and using that acronym to help you better understand some of the triggers in your life that can lead to poor decisions.

With temptation, it is not a matter of "if" you will be tempted, it is "when" and how often you will be tempted. This is such an important word to understand and know what a devastating impact if can have in your life and on your family if you yield to temptation.

What are some of the common temptations? Sex outside of marriage, Alcohol and Drug consumption, over eating, etc.

How can you avoid being tempted to have Sex outside of marriage? You can start by not allowing yourself to be put in situations where you are alone with someone of the opposite sex. You can be very circumspect about who you interact with on social media. Don't make any decision regarding your relationship if you are Hungry, Angry, Lonely or Tired.

One of the things we discuss at length with our children is the evils of illicit drug use and the effects if can have on your family and your health. We discuss that if you never try drugs, then you have a ZERO percent chance of becoming an addict. If you never try alcohol, then you have a ZERO percent chance of becoming an alcoholic. We tell them to never let these things get a "toe hold" in their life.

How do we avoid these kinds of temptations?   We don't have these things present in our home, we don't frequent bars or taverns where the sole purpose is alcohol consumption, we have friends and peer group who have the same thoughts and values that we have.   We walk the talk in front of our children.

It is important to be prepared and know what you are going to do before you are tempted, because in the moment you may not be thinking clearly. Decide now what your answer or action will be when temptation arises and tries to enter your life.

The point of this chapter is that we should not ignore temptation, nor fear temptation, but be prepared to act when temptation comes at us (see verses below as a good starting point).

Homework - Read these verses below and memorize them.   Lean into God and his word to give you the strength and wisdom you will need to conquer the temptations in your life.

1 Corinthians 10:13
No temptation has overtaken you but such as is common to man; and God is faithful, who will not allow you to be tempted beyond what you are able, but with the temptation will provide the way of escape also, so that you will be able to endure it.

Matthew 26:41
Keep watching and praying that you may not enter into temptation; the spirit is willing, but the flesh is weak."

Ephesians 6:11
Put on the full armor of God, so that you will be able to stand firm against the schemes of the devil.

Trials

"Trials teach us what we are; they dig up the soil, and let us see what we are made of." **Charles Spurgeon**

<u>Definition - Trial</u> - a test of the quality, value, or usefulness of something

What stories do we like to read about?   We are all inspired about people who overcame incredible trials in their life and went on to do great things.

Bethany Hamilton - she had her arm bitten off by a shark while surfing. We might never have ever heard about her if this had not happened, but she went on to be incredibly successful and it has opened many doors for her to share her faith and have a positive impact on peoples lives.

I do not know anybody who would willingly ask for trials in their life! If given a choice at the time, I doubt Bethany Hamilton would have chosen to have her arm bitten off by a shark.

Just as in the previous chapter, it is not a question of "if" you will have trials in your life, but "when" will you have trials in your life.

I have heard is said many times that people are either heading into a trial, in the middle of a trial or coming out of a trial in their life.   Boy, has this been true in our life.

It is the summer of 2014 and we are in the middle of a trial in our lives with one of our children.   We are administering some "tough love" and nobody told us how tough it would be on us!!   Our prayer is that we would be faithful through this entire process and be able to speak into other family's lives if they have a similar situation.

It is the height of Christian maturity to be able to look back on the trials in your life and see how God used them to grow you and bring you closer to Him.

It may seem a bit odd to have this word in the top 100 words, but if we are honest and look at the entirety of our lives, we will look back at those times when we had trials and see those as inflection points in our lives.

How deep is our faith in God, our trust in God, and our relationship with God? See verse below.

Homework - How do you prepare for a trial? Draw close to God now and improve your relationship with him. The stronger your relationship with God, the great chance you will have to endure the trial and see God's great wisdom and plan (BTW - we may not always understand or know God's plan or design - so it is important to trust Him, even when we do not understand).

James 1:2-4
Consider it all joy, my brethren, when you encounter various trials, knowing that the testing of your faith produces endurance. And let endurance have its perfect result, so that you may be perfect and complete, lacking in nothing.

Distractions

"By prevailing over all obstacles and distractions, one may unfailingly arrive at his chosen goal or destination."
Christopher Columbus

Definition - Distraction - something that makes it difficult to think or pay attention

Distractions are all around us. They keep us from focusing on what we need to do and where we need to go.

When I was in Las Vegas for a convention, there were distractions everywhere. The entire city is a complete distraction from reality.

In my hotel, at the very lobby there was a juggler to grab your attention. I stopped and watched for a few minutes. Then I noticed that about 20 feet further into the casino floor there was a different group of performers and still further in an additional group. It hit me in that instance that the very objective of each of these groups was to "suck me in" and distract me and get me to the casino floor.

There will always be distractions in life! It is our job to ignore the distractions and stay the course. In the chapters to follow you will see that I talk about the need to manage, plan, focus and have a vision. You must have a plan to know where you are going, or else the distraction of the world will forever keep you from reaching your destination.

Here are some key distractions to consider:

Television
Sports (both viewing and participation)
Hobbies (Hunting, fishing, racing)
Cell Phone

Social Networks
Video Games

To be clear, none of these things listed is a "bad", but how much of a distraction are they in your life? Do you control them or do they control you? Be honest with yourself.

Homework – take the time this week to list all of the distractions in your life. Were you surprised by how many there are.

Matthew 14:28-31

Peter said to Him, "Lord, if it is You, command me to come to You on the water." And He said, "Come!" And Peter got out of the boat, and walked on the water and came toward Jesus. But seeing the wind, he became frightened, and beginning to sink, he cried out, "Lord, save me!" Immediately Jesus stretched out His hand and took hold of him, and said to him, "You of little faith, why did you doubt?"

Guard

"One is not exposed to danger who, even when in safety is always on their guard." **Publilius Syrus**

<u>Definition - Guard</u> - a state in which someone is carefully looking for possible danger, threats, problems, etc

There are three key areas of your life that you must guard:

- You must guard your eyes (beware of what you look at – on-line, TV, magazines and live).

- You must guard your mind (beware of evil thoughts and desires).

- You must guard your heart (because life flows from your heart).

What are the dangers of dropping your guard? What is the military punishment for sleeping on guard duty?

> *Maximum punishment.*
>
> *(1) In time of war. Death or such other punishment as a court-martial may direct.*
>
> *(2) While receiving special pay under 37 U.S.C. § 310. Dishonorable discharge, forfeiture of all pay and allowances, and confinement for 10 years.*
>
> *(3) In all other places. Dishonorable discharge, forfeiture of all pay and allowances, and confinement for 1 year*

Death! Really!

Yes, falling asleep on guard duty could and did in many instances lead to the death penalty. It was not just the life of the guard that was in danger when he fell asleep, but the lives of all the men in the camp.

You see , when we let our guard down, we are in danger not only for our life, but for those we are guarding.

Who do we guard? Our spouse, our children and our family.

Consider the danger and the consequences of letting your guard down and falling into temptation and sin.

<u>Homework</u> – put your guard up and keep it up! Guard your eyes, mind and guard your heart..

Proverbs 2:11
Discretion will guard you, Understanding will watch over you,

Luke 12:15
Then He said to them, "Beware, and be on your guard against every form of greed; for not even when one has an abundance does his life consist of his possessions."

Luke 21:34
"Be on guard, so that your hearts will not be weighted down with dissipation and drunkenness and the worries of life, and that day will not come on you suddenly like a trap;

Proverbs 4:23
Watch over your heart with all diligence,
For from it flow the springs of life.

Flee

"I know well what I am fleeing from but not what I am in search of".
Michel de Montaigne

<u>Definition - Flee</u> - to run away from danger

Read these three bible verses below. It is a very simple lesson to read, but sometimes more difficult to execute.

I would advocate that you need to be prepared with your plan before you are confronted with a situation where you might have to flee. Know what your answer will be before you encounter these situations. You cannot wait to be hit with temptation and then decide what the right thing to do is at that point.

When my Bride and I went to a Broadway play (that was highly recommended), it became clear within the first 5 minutes that we had no business being there. I grabbed my Brides hand and we immediately left. You see, we had both decided a long time ago that when we saw something objectionable, we would not stay and watch, but have the courage to get up and walk out.

This is why it is important to hide God's word in your heart and let it be a lamp unto your feet and light upon your path. God's word is filled with the wisdom and knowledge that you need to know how to deal with every kind of sin and temptation.

Remember, it is not enough to just know, you must be willing to act!

<u>Homework</u> – is there anything you should be fleeing from right now? Examine your life and if you need to flee, then flee!

2 Timothy 2:22

Now flee from youthful lusts and pursue righteousness, faith, love and peace, with those who call on the Lord from a pure heart.
I wanted to start

1 Corinthians 10:13

No temptation has overtaken you but such as is common to man; and God is faithful, who will not allow you to be tempted beyond what you are able, but with the temptation will provide the way of escape also, so that you will be able to endure it.

Genesis 39:11-12

Now it happened one day that he **(Joseph)** *went into the house to do his work, and none of the men of the household was there inside. She* **(Potiphar's Wife)** *caught him by his garment, saying, "Lie with me!" And he left his garment in her hand and fled, and went outside.*

Fear

"Only Thing We Have to Fear Is Fear Itself": **FDR**

<u>Homework</u> - Read these verses below and memorize them. Lean into God and his word to give you the strength and wisdom you will need to conquer the temptations in your life.

<u>Definition - Fear</u> - to be afraid of (something or someone)

God has not called us to fear, but to trust and obey Him. With that said, we all have things we fear.

The Book of Lists reports the Top Ten Human Fears as:

1. Speaking before a Group
2. Heights
3. Insects and bugs
4. Financial problems
5. Deep water
6. Sickness
7. Death
8. Flying
9. Loneliness
10. Dogs

There may be something on this list that resonates with you and possibly makes you cringe. However, bravery is not the complete absence of fear, but the willingness to move forward in spite of the fear.

We must be willing to put our trust in the Lord and have Him lead, guide and direct our lives. We must be a positive example to our spouse and to our children and not show fear, but trust and believe in God and his goodness and grace for our lives.

Homework – if you have fear in your life, confess it to God and ask Him to help you overcome your fears.   Seek wise counsel from others who may have overcome these same fears.

2 Timothy 1:7

*For God has not given us a spirit of timidity (**fear**), but of power and love and discipline.*

1 John 4:18

There is no fear in love; but perfect love casts out fear, because fear involves punishment, and the one who fears is not perfected in love.

Psalm 56:3-4

When I am afraid,
I will put my trust in You.
In God, whose word I praise,
In God I have put my trust;
I shall not be afraid.
What can mere man do to me?

Romans 8:31

What then shall we say to these things? If God is for us, who is against us?

Boldness

"Fortune favours the bold." **Virgil**

"Boldness be my friend." **William Shakespeare**

<u>Definition - Bold</u> - not afraid of danger or difficult situations

I added this word to my list after a mission trip to Africa.

My daughters and I went to Cape Verde, West Africa on a mission trip with our church and it was an incredible two weeks in the field. Most of the believers on the island were fairly new Christians and were very excited about the opportunity to evangelize and share the gospel.

I was amazed at their boldness and quite frankly put to shame! They had no hesitation to walk up to strangers and share the good news. They boldly walked into a bar or home and shared their testimony. I was so encouraged and so blessed by their boldness, that my own boldness increased and by the time we left, I felt as bold as them.

God did not call us to be timid, but to boldly share the good news of the Gospel of Jesus Christ. This is the type of boldness that I desire for my children to have and for me to continue to model for them.

<u>Homework</u> – go this week and boldly share the Gospel with your family or co-workers.

<u>Psalm 138:3</u>
On the day I called, You answered me; You made me bold with strength in my soul.

Ephesians 3:11-12

This was in accordance with the eternal purpose which He carried out in Christ Jesus our Lord, in whom we have boldness and confident access through faith in Him.

Ephesians 6:18-20

With all prayer and petition pray at all times in the Spirit, and with this in view, be on the alert with all perseverance and petition for all the saints, and pray on my behalf, that utterance may be given to me in the opening of my mouth, to make known with boldness the mystery of the gospel, for which I am an ambassador in chains; that in proclaiming it I may speak boldly, as I ought to speak

Truth

"If you tell the truth, you don't have to remember anything."
Mark Twain

<u>Definition - Truth</u> - the real facts about something : the things that are true

Without the truth there can be not trust. Without trust there can be no healthy relationships.

In the context of this book there are two truths:

- Telling the truth (as in do not tell a lie).

- Jesus is the truth

We must have both aspects of truth in our life to have the relationships that make life worth living - a relationship with Christ and a relationship with our spouse and children.

Do not think that truthfulness is a license to be blunt or rude. Tact is still a very important characteristic and should govern polite conversation. Just because an overweight person walks into the room does not mean you tell them they are fat. Is it a fact that they are fat? Yes. Have they asked your opinion or sought your advice on their physical appearance? No. Therefore, keep your thoughts to yourself.

Also, do not confuse Truth with opinion. Too many times, people will offer an opinion veiled as truth and will potentially harm a relationship. Remember, opinions are like noses, everyone has one.

Example of opinion –vs- Fact/Truth

Opinion – It is cold in the room

Fact/Truth – It is 65 degrees in the room (some may think it is cold and others comfortable but the truth is that it is 65 degrees)

Should you always tell the truth? The answer is yes! Some would say philosophically that it is appropriate to lie at times (situational lying). I would advocate that it would be better to just keep your mouth shut and not say anything. Silence can be a very effective form of communication.

<u>Homework</u> – make truthfulness a key character quality of your life and teach it to your children.

Proverbs 3:3
Do not let kindness and truth leave you; Bind them around your neck, Write them on the tablet of your heart.

Psalm 86:11
Teach me Your way, O Lord; I will walk in Your truth; Unite my heart to fear Your name.

John 8:31-32
So Jesus was saying to those Jews who had believed Him, "If you continue in My word, then you are truly disciples of Mine; and you will know the truth, and the truth will make you free."

John 14:6
Jesus said to him, "I am the way, and the truth, and the life; no one comes to the Father but through Me.

3 John 1:4
I have no greater joy than this, to hear of my children walking in the truth.

Unity

"Where there is unity there is always victory." **Publilius Syrus**

"If we do not hang together, we shall surely hang separately."
Benjamin Franklin

<u>Definition - Unity</u> - the state of being in full agreement

I love the quote above from Benjamin Franklin. This was not mere
rhetoric from one of the greatest men of his time. He and the fellow
signers of the Declaration of Independence were committing treason, and
the punishment for treason was hanging. They were risking their lives
and their fortunes on the fate of the American Revolution.

It is a basic tenet of war, that to defeat your enemy, you must divide and
conquer. In other words, attack where you enemy is weakest and seek to
destroy him piece by piece.

However, when there is unity of purpose, unity of thought, unity of action,
then there is no area of weakness for the enemy to attack.

Unity demands humility, communication and trust. Without these three
characteristics, it is almost impossible to have Unity. Without humility
then the egos take over, without communication then disorganization
takes over and without trust, bitterness and caution crush the spirit of
unity.

Unity at church is supreme to get anything meaningful accomplished.
The same is true in your family. You must be unified as a family and
understand your purpose.

A chain is only as strong as its weakest link.

<u>Homework</u> – do you have unity in your church? Unity in your home? If not, are you the weak link? Work on bringing unity into your life this week.

Philippians 2:1-2

Therefore if there is any encouragement in Christ, if there is any consolation of love, if there is any fellowship of the Spirit, if any affection and compassion, make my joy complete by being of the same mind, maintaining the same love, united in spirit, intent on one purpose.

1 Corinthians 1:10

Now I exhort you, brethren, by the name of our Lord Jesus Christ, that you all agree and that there be no divisions among you, but that you be made complete in the same mind and in the same judgment.

Colossians 3:14

Beyond all these things put on love, which is the perfect bond of unity.

Worship

"Worship is an it-is-well-with-my-soul experience." -
Robert Webber

Definition - Worship - the act of showing respect and love for a god especially by praying with other people who believe in the same god : the act of worshipping God or a god

Worship is not something that is only done at church on Sunday. Now certainly we should have corporate Worship at church on Sunday and there is nothing sweeter that praising and worshiping God with other believers.

However, we can worship God wherever we are and in any situation. We hear stories of believers in jail worshiping God. We hear of believers in desperate situations worshiping God. You can have your own time of worship sitting in your car, or in the tub, or while flying in an airplane. Worship is not based on the location; it is based on the attitude of the heart.

Homework – look for ways this week to worship God sometime other than Sunday at church.

Psalm 2:11
Worship the Lord with reverence And rejoice with trembling

Psalm 66:4
"All the earth will worship You, And will sing praises to You; They will sing praises to Your name." Selah

Matthew 2:2

"Where is He who has been born King of the Jews? For we saw His star in the east and have come to worship Him."

Luke 4:8

Jesus answered him, "It is written, 'You shall worship the Lord your God and serve Him only.'"

Deuteronomy 6:13

You shall fear only the Lord your God; and you shall worship Him and swear by His name.

Praise

"The sweetest of all sounds is praise." **Xenophon**

<u>Definition - Praise</u> - to say or write good things about (someone or something) : to express approval of (someone or something): to express thanks to or love and respect for (God)

Praise in this context really has two meanings.   Praising others and praising God.

We need to praise one another.   My Bride needs praise as do my children. My children crave praise (as do all children).   How often do we hear our children shouting out "look at me", "watch me". They are looking for our approval and our praise.

Praise is like oxygen to a suffocating man. He can never get enough of it.

In this same way, we should praise God. Many times we may find it difficult (if not impossible) to praise God when we are in the middle of a storm. However, it has been my personal experience that we can never see any situation end to end and it is better to praise God, even though we do not understand.

<u>Homework</u> - Read Psalm 150 below and think about how you can praise God.

<u>Psalm 150</u>
Praise the Lord!
Praise God in His sanctuary;
Praise Him in His mighty expanse.

Praise Him for His mighty deeds;
Praise Him according to His excellent greatness.
Praise Him with trumpet sound;
Praise Him with harp and lyre.
Praise Him with timbrel and dancing;
Praise Him with stringed instruments and pipe.
Praise Him with loud cymbals;
Praise Him with resounding cymbals.
Let everything that has breath praise the Lord.
Praise the Lord!

Pray

"*Work as if you were to live a hundred years. Pray as if you were to die tomorrow*". **Benjamin Franklin**

<u>Definition - Pray </u>- to speak to God especially in order to give thanks or to ask for something

Prayer can and does change lives! God hears our prayers and answers in His timing. I have heard it said that there are three types of answers to a prayer – yes, no and not yet.   I would argue that there are only two answers to prayer – yes or no.   We are not wise enough to know when the answer is "not yet".

I have seen first hand how prayer has changed others' lives and how it has changed my life.   I have seen answered prayers time and time again.

Prayer is one of the few offensive weapons in the Christians life.   We use prayer to speak directly to God and to seek His wisdom and guidance and to lift up others who are in need.

I have my prayer journal where I keep up with regular/daily prayers:

Bride, children, family, close friends, church etc.

I then add to my daily prayers, any special prayer requests:

Healing for the sick, need for wisdom or guidance for specific situations etc.

We have a regular routine of prayer as a family and prayer by ourselves. As a matter of fact I have prayed over this book and I pray that it can and will touch lives.

Pray is a foundational element of the Christian life!!

Homework – If you do not already have a prayer journal, go to the store an purchase a journal and start a regular routine of prayer.

1 Thessalonians 5:17
pray without ceasing;

James 5:16
Therefore, confess your sins to one another, and pray for one another so that you may be healed. The effective prayer of a righteous man can accomplish much.

Philippians 4:6
Be anxious for nothing, but in everything by prayer and supplication with thanksgiving let your requests be made known to God.

Mark 11:24
Therefore I say to you, all things for which you pray and ask, believe that you have received them, and they will be granted you.

Matthew 6:9-13
"Pray, then, in this way:
'Our Father who is in heaven,
Hallowed be Your name.
'Your kingdom come.
Your will be done,
On earth as it is in heaven.
'Give us this day [a]our daily bread.
'And forgive us our debts, as we also have forgiven our debtors.
'And do not lead us into temptation, but deliver us from]evil. [For Yours is the kingdom and the power and the glory forever. Amen.']

Bless/Blessings

"I think in every lesson there's a blessing, and there's so many blessings from all the lessons I've had to go through in life."
Alonzo Mourning

<u>Definition - Bless</u> - to ask God to care for and protect (someone or something): to provide (a person, place, etc.) with something good or desirable

We constantly teach our children about God's blessings in our lives and how we should be thankful for the way that God blesses us.

We do not need to look far for Gods blessing, they are all around us if we just open our hearts and minds.

The air we breathe, the sun that shines, the very earth we live on. These are all blessing from God.

Not only do we receive blessing from God, but we should bless others as well.

My Bride and I are constantly looking for ways to bless our children! My oldest daughter Hannah is preparing to go away to college and she is working very hard to save her money (we require all of your children to work and have "skin in the game").

As she is saving her money and diligently putting it aside, we look for ways to bless her because of her obedience and diligence. This week, we paid part of her car insurance (normally she pays 100% of this). If she continues with her savings and reaches her goal, then we are going to replace her broken cell phone (again this is something that she is 100% responsible for, but we want to bless her).

We are constantly looking for ways to bless our children and I believe that God (as a good father) is constantly looking for ways to bless us when we are obedient and diligent.

God has blessed me with an incredible Bride and because of that, I am a rich man indeed!

<u>Homework</u> – chose this week to see Gods blessing in your life and chose to bless others.

Genesis 12:2

And I will make you a great nation, And I will bless you, And make your name great; And so you shall be a blessing;

Genesis 22:17

indeed I will greatly bless you, and I will greatly multiply your seed as the stars of the heavens and as the sand which is on the seashore; and your seed shall possess the gate of their enemies.

Psalm 115:15

May you be blessed of the Lord, Maker of heaven and earth.

Psalm 134:3

May the Lord bless you from Zion, He who made heaven and earth.

Holy

"*Holiness, not happiness, is the chief end of man.*" **Oswald Chambers**

<u>Definition - Holy</u> - exalted or worthy of complete devotion as one perfect in goodness and righteousness

God is calling us to be holy, because he is holy.   When we think of Gods character, we typically think of Love.   But before love, God is Holy.

Holiness is only possible through a personal relationship with Jesus.   Jesus said "I am the way, the truth and the life. No man comes to the Father but through Me".   It is impossible for us to be holy without that personal relationship with Christ.

We should desire to be holy, because that is one of the characteristics that God used to describe himself.

<u>Homework</u> – look up all the words in the bible for Holy and reflect on Gods holiness.   See some of the verses below.

<u>Leviticus 11:44</u>
For I am the Lord your God. Consecrate yourselves therefore, and be holy, for I am holy

<u>Isaiah 6:3</u>
And one called out to another and said, "Holy, Holy, Holy, is the Lord of hosts, The whole earth is full of His glory."

1 Peter 1:14-16

As obedient children, do not be conformed to the former lusts which were yours in your ignorance, but like the Holy One who called you, be holy yourselves also in all your behavior; because it is written, "You shall be holy, for I am holy."

Sin

"*Sin will take you farther than you want to go, keep you longer than you planned to stay, and cost you more than you thought*" -
Johnny Hunt

"*One leak will sink a ship, and one sin will destroy a sinner.*"
John Bunyan

<u>Definition - Sin</u> - an offense against religious or moral law

Why is sin one of the most important words? Because sin is evident in everyone's life! Sin has the power to destroy individuals and families.

These next three chapters go together. Please read them as one and know that all three of these words (Sin, Repentance and Salvation) are all key words in the Christian life.

<u>Homework</u> – if there is sin in your life, confess it to God, repent and turn from your sin.

<u>**Romans 3:23**</u>
for all have sinned and fall short of the glory of God,

Psalm 51:2

Wash me thoroughly from my iniquity And cleanse me from my sin.

Psalm 32:3

When I kept silent about my sin, my body wasted away Through my groaning all day long.

Psalm 32:5

I acknowledged my sin to You, And my iniquity I did not hide; I said, "I will confess my transgressions to the Lord"; And You forgave the guilt of my sin. Selah.

John 8:34

Jesus answered them, "Truly, truly, I say to you, everyone who commits sin is the slave of sin.

Repent

"Only through repentance and faith in Christ can anyone be saved. No religious activity will be sufficient, only true faith in Jesus Christ alone." **Ravi Zacharias**

<u>Definition - Repent </u>- to feel or show that you are sorry for something bad or wrong that you did and that you want to do what is right

Repentance is key to the Christian life. We must examine our lives on a continual basis and confess our sin to God and turn from that sin. Repentance is turning from that sin and life style. There can be no salvation without repentance (see next chapter)

<u>Homework</u> – if there are any areas of your life you need to repent, then take the opportunity to confess your sin to God today.

<u>Mark 1:14-16</u>
Now after John had been taken into custody, Jesus came into Galilee, preaching the gospel of God, and saying, "The time is fulfilled, and the kingdom of God is at hand; repent and believe in the gospel."

<u>Luke 5:31-33</u>
And Jesus answered and said to them, "It is not those who are well who need a physician, but those who are sick. I have not come to call the righteous but sinners to repentance."

Acts 3:

Therefore repent and return, so that your sins may be wiped away, in order that times of refreshing may come from the presence of the Lord;

Luke 24:46-48

and He said to them, "Thus it is written, that the Christ would suffer and rise again from the dead the third day, and that repentance for forgiveness of sins would be proclaimed in His name to all the nations, beginning from Jerusalem. You are witnesses of these things.

Luke 13:2-6

And Jesus said to them, "Do you suppose that these Galileans were greater sinners than all other Galileans because they suffered this fate? I tell you, no, but unless you repent, you will all likewise perish. Or do you suppose that those eighteen on whom the tower in Siloam fell and killed them were worse culprits than all the men who live in Jerusalem? I tell you, no, but unless you repent, you will all likewise perish."

Salvation

"The first step in a person's salvation is knowledge of their sin"
Lucius Annaeus Seneca

<u>Definition - Salvation</u> - the act of saving someone from sin or evil : the state of being saved from sin or evil

For this chapter, I simply want to refer you to the "Romans Road"

Who is good?
"As it is written, There is none righteous, no, not one."
Romans 3:10

Who has sinned?
"For all have sinned, and come short of the glory of God."
Romans 3:23

Where sin comes from:
"Wherefore, as by one man sin entered into the world, and death by sin; and so death passed upon all men, for that all have sinned."
Romans 5:12

God's price for sin:
"For the wages of sin is death; but the gift of God is eternal life through Jesus Christ our Lord." Romans 6:23

Our way to salvation:
"But God commendeth His love toward us, in that while we were yet sinners, Christ died for us." Romans 5:8

"That if thou shalt confess with thy mouth the Lord Jesus, and shalt believe in thine heart that God hath raised Him from the dead, thou shalt be saved." Romans 10:9

"For whosoever shall call upon the name of the Lord shall be saved."
Romans 10:13

<u>Homework</u> - share the Romans Road -(God's path for salivation) – with someone this week.

Psalm 18:2
The Lord is my rock and my fortress and my deliverer, My God, my rock, in whom I take refuge; My shield and the horn of my salvation, my stronghold.

John 3:16-17
"For God so loved the world, that He gave His [a]only begotten Son, that whoever believes in Him shall not perish, but have eternal life. For God did not send the Son into the world to judge the world, but that the world might be saved through Him.

Romans 10:8-10
But what does it say? "The word is near you, in your mouth and in your heart" – that is, the word of faith which we are preaching, that if you confess with your mouth Jesus as Lord, and believe in your heart that God raised Him from the dead, you will be saved; for with the heart a person believes, resulting in righteousness, and with the mouth he confesses, resulting in salvation.

Purity

"Purity does not mean crushing the instincts but having the instincts as servants and not the master of the spirit."
Eric Liddell

<u>Definition - Purity</u> - lack of guilt or evil thoughts

Ivory soap - 99 44/100% pure. Many people think of Ivory Soap as "pure" soap, and yet it is not 100% pure. There is a little something left over that prevents the soap from being 100% pure.

Pure Gold seldom comes out of the ground as 100% pure. It must be refined in the fire and melted down and have all of the impurities removed before it is 100% pure gold. In other words, it takes some action to make gold 100% pure.

In this same way our lives are not 100% pure without Christ! God desires us to have purity of thought and purity of action. Without Christ, this is impossible, but through Christ all things are possible. In the old testament when a sacrifice was needed, the looked for a "spotless" or pure lamb to sacrifice and atone for the sins. Christ was the pure and spotless lamb that was sacrificed for our sins.

Many think of purity only in the physical sense of being pure for your wedding day. However, Christ has already told us that even if our thoughts are impure, it is as if we have committed the sinful acts. God is much more concerned about us having a pure heart, because from the heart flows the actions, attitude and choices we make in life.

Purity should be the goal for every boy and girl, and every man and woman. I find that my thoughts and deeds are not pure when I am not close to God. The more time I spend in his word, the more time I spend in worship and praise, the more closely my thoughts, deeds and actions begin to reflect Christ.

We just finished the words on Sin, Repentance and Salvation. Purity is the next logical step in the Christian faith. God desires us to be pure and for purity to be a key attribute in our life. Teach it to yourself, and model it for your spouse and children.

Homework – examine your life for areas of impurity and ask Christ to forgive you and turn from your impure ways. Turn to Christ and seek purity through your relationship with Him.

Psalm 1:9
How can a young man keep his way pure?
By keeping it according to Your word.

Matthew 5:8
"Blessed are the pure in heart, for they shall see God.

Yoked

"The yoke you wear determines the burden you bear."
Edwin Louis Cole

<u>Definition - Yoke</u> - a bar or frame that is attached to the heads or necks of two work animals (such as oxen) so that they can pull a plow or heavy load

This may seem like an odd word to many of you who are not familiar with all of its meaning. If I was to say Yoke or Yoked, most people think of an egg.

But the definition above is the one that I am referring to.

What would happen if you were to yoke together an Ox and a Mule? What would happen is that the stronger of the two would pull the other in the direction they wanted to go instead of going in the same direction and both pulling the load equally!

From an early age, we have taught our children the importance of pursuing a relationship only with a fellow Christian. We follow 2 Corinthians 6:14 (see below) and what it says about our relationship with unbelievers in regards to dating and marriage.

2 Corinthians 6:14
Do not be unequally yoked together with unbelievers; for what partnership have righteousness and lawlessness, or what fellowship has light with darkness?

 We do not believe in "missionary dating"! What is missionary dating? It is dating someone with the belief that we can lead them to a personal relationship with Christ.

The most important decision anyone will make in their lives is the decision to accept Christ as their personal Lord and Savior. The second most important decision is who they will marry.

Because of the importance of this marriage decision and ramification it has for an entire lives, we believe teaching our children about the word Yoked and its implications is incredibly important.

Homework - study this verse and see how it speaks into your life. Commit today for you and your family to be yoked together with only believers.

Expectations

"High expectations are the key to everything." **Sam Walton**

"You can expect what you inspect." **Edwards Deming**

<u>Definition - Expectation</u> - a belief that something will happen or is likely to happen: a feeling or belief about how successful, good, etc., someone or something will be

I tell my children all the time that I have a great definition for frustration.

Frustration lies between expectations and reality. You expect one thing and get another. Thus you get frustrated. I expect to have beautiful weather for my vacation at the beach, but instead, it rains every day. I then get frustrated.

We all have expectations of ourselves and of others. Our focus is on having and setting realistic expectations for all areas of our life (spiritual, financial, relational, emotional, or physical)

I am a big believer in "you can expect what you inspect". This is especially true with my children. When we set expectations and then do not follow through with inspection, then my children may not believe that the expectation was real. If my expectation is for them to clean their room and I never go to their room to see how well they have done, then they might not believe this is a real expectation (this is also a good opportunity to offer praise for a job well done or discipline for a job done poorly).

Do you have realistic expectations for your life, your spouse or your children? If not, why not?

<u>Homework</u> – Make a list of expectations you have all areas of your life spiritual, financial, relational, emotional, or physical).

<u>Philippians 1:-21</u>

for I know that this will turn out for my deliverance through your prayers and the provision of the Spirit of Jesus Christ, according to my earnest expectation and hope, that I will not be put to shame in anything, but that with all boldness, Christ will even now, as always, be exalted in my body, whether by life or by death.
For to me, to live is Christ and to die is gain.

Plan

"He who fails to plan is planning to fail" **Winston Churchill**

<u>Definition - Plan</u> - a set of actions that have been thought of as a way to do or achieve something

I have my own saying that I have taught my children:

"Have a plan and work your plan" **Paul Beersdorf**

We cannot go through life by happenstance! That is a recipe for disaster.

I work for a Fortune 100 company, and for us, we have what we call "continuous planning". This means we are constantly reviewing the plan on a weekly basis and making adjustments as necessary.

I have had several job titles at work that have had the title "Planning Manager, Planning Development, etc." Our company knows and believes that planning is incredibly important and that we will not be successful without it.

God has plans for our lives:

Jeremiah 29:11
For I know the plans that I have for you,' declares the Lord, 'plans for welfare and not for calamity to give you a future and a hope.

God wants us to commit our work and plans to him:

Proverbs 16:3
Commit your works to the Lord
And your plans will be established.

God want to be very thoughtful with our plans and planning:

Proverbs 21:5 .
The plans of the diligent lead surely to advantage,
But everyone who is hasty comes surely to poverty.

Do you plan?

Do you have a plan for the following:

How you will spend your time?
How you will invest your money?
How you will use your talents (your skills and abilities)?
etc.
etc.

Homework - There are so many areas of your life that you can and should have plans for.   If you do not have plans, start today with a plan on how to use your time.   Think about this coming week and how you will use your time to have a positive impact on others and encourage them!

Goals

"When it is obvious that the goals cannot be reached, don't adjust the goals, adjust the action steps." **Confucius**

<u>Definition - Goal</u> - something that you are trying to do or achieve

I am a huge believer in goals and goal setting. I believe that you must write you goals down and be accountable to someone if you really want to achieve them.

The best method I have found is SMART goals. S.M.A.R.T goals means, Specific, Measurable, Actionable, Reasonable and Time Bound.

I want to juxtapose examples of non-smart goals and SMART goals. We will assume this family makes $60,000 per year and has one son who is 8 years old

Non-smart goal

We want to save money for college.

While this may sound good, it is too vague, not measurable, not time-bound.

SMART goal

We want to save $20,000 over the next 10 years for our son's college expenses. We will save $167 each month starting next month and invest the money in a 529 savings plan.

This goal meets all of the criteria to be a SMART goal

Specific – Money for son's college into a 529 plan

Measurable - $20,000 (or $167 each month)

Actionable – start next month

Reasonable – on a monthly basis this is about 3.3% of their income.

Time-bound – each month for the next 10 years

This was a fairly easy example of a financial goal, but goal setting can be used in every aspect of your life – spiritual, financial, relational, emotional and physical. Using goals and goal setting is a way of life and is a learned skill. Just because you never used goals before is not an excuse for not using them now.

<u>Homework</u> – start today and use the SMART method of goal setting for your life. Make sure you have someone holding you accountable to your goals.

Philippians 3:13-14
Brethren, I do not regard myself as having laid hold of it yet; but one thing I do: forgetting what lies behind and reaching forward to what lies ahead, I press on toward the goal for the prize of the upward call of God in Christ Jesus.

1 Timothy 1:5
But the goal of our instruction is love from a pure heart and a good conscience and a sincere faith.

Focus

"Concentrate all your thoughts upon the work at hand. The sun's rays do not burn until brought to a focus."
Alexander Graham Bell

<u>Definition - Focus</u> - a subject that is being discussed or studied: the subject on which people's attention is focused

Focus is all about the allocation of resources. What in the world do I mean by that?

We only have so many resources available at our disposal. Namely - Time, Talents and Treasure. These are all valuable assets, but for most of us they are not in abundant supply. Therefore, we must focus our assets to get the biggest return on investment.

I know a young man who wanted to become a great musician, artist and actor. He sought the council of some wise older associates and they all told him the same thing; he must choose one of these areas and focus all of his resources on developing that area of his life.

I read in the book Outliers (by Malcolm Gladwell) that it takes 10,000 hours for someone to become an expert. When you think about it, that makes a lot of sense. 10,000 hours is the equivalent of 4 years working 50 hours per week.   To become a licensed plumber or electrician usually takes about 4 years. A college bachelor's degree is a four year program. Medical School is 4 years (plus under graduate, residency and fellowships).

In other words, focus is absolutely necessary to complete a given task. Without focus, we are directionless and therefore useless.

<u>Homework</u> – take one aspect of your life (spiritual, financial, relational, emotional, or physical) this week and focus on improving in that area.

Romans 12:2
And do not be conformed to this world, but be transformed by the renewing of your mind, so that you may prove what the will of God is, that which is good and acceptable and perfect.

Work

"There is no substitute for hard work." **Thomas Edison**

"The only place success comes before work is in the dictionary."
Vince Lombardi

<u>Definition - Work</u> - activity in which one exerts strength or faculties to do
or perform something:

I have had a job since I was 9 years old. I only know work and working
and have seen the fruition of my labors.

It was very important for us to convey working hard and earning an
income early for our children. We could have provided them with
everything, but we felt the more important lesson was for them to be hard
workers!

Our children always had jobs and chores at home, but when our children
turned 16, we required them to get a "real" job.   You see, we told them
that if they wanted a cell phone, car, movie admission etc.. That it would
be their responsibility to earn the money to pay for those things. In other
words we wanted our children to have "skin in the game".

Since that time they have purchased their own cars, cell phones, insurance,
clothes and even their own vacations and time away.   We can see the
pride they have received in having to work for someone else, and as a
father, I love to see my children cleaning the public bathroom and
mopping the entire restaurant as part of their job.

When we talk to them about hard work, we also talk about school work,
work they do for the church, work at home and work done on mission
trips.

<u>Homework</u> – it is never wrong to work hard! If you are not working hard in all aspects of your life, then ask yourself why and seek to remedy the situation.   Choose to be a good example of hard worker for your spouse and children.

Colossians 3:23
Whatever you do, do your work heartily, as for the Lord rather than for men,

Proverbs 16:3
Commit your works to the Lord
And your plans will be established.

Ephesians 4:28
He who steals must steal no longer; but rather he must labor, performing with his own hands what is good, so that he will have something to share with one who has need.

Manage

"When you can't solve the problem, manage it"
Robert H. Schuller

<u>Definition - **Manage**</u> - to take care of and make decisions about (someone's time, money, etc.

In Matthew25: 14-28, Jesus teaches the parable of the Talents.   The three servants are given money to manage for their master. Two of them do a great job and the third fails completely.

[14] "For *it is* just like a man *about* to go on a journey, who called his own slaves and entrusted his possessions to them. [15] To one he gave five talents, to another, two, and to another, one, each according to his own ability; and he went on his journey.[16] Immediately the one who had received the five talents went and traded with them, and gained five more talents. [17] In the same manner the one who *had received* the two *talents* gained two more. [18] But he who received the one *talent* went away, and dug *a hole* in the ground and hid his [b]master's money.

"Now after a long time the master of those slaves *came and *settled accounts with them. [20] The one who had received the five talents came up and brought five more talents, saying, 'Master, you entrusted five talents to me. See, I have gained five more talents.' [21] His master said to him, 'Well done, good and faithful slave. You were faithful with a few things, I will put you in charge of many things; enter into the joy of your master.'

22 "Also the one who *had received* the two talents came up and said, 'Master, you entrusted two talents to me. See, I have gained two more talents.' 23 His master said to him, 'Well done, good and faithful slave. You were faithful with a few things, I will put you in charge of many things; enter into the joy of your master.'

24 "And the one also who had received the one talent came up and said, 'Master, I knew you to be a hard man, reaping where you did not sow and gathering where you scattered no *seed*. 25 And I was afraid, and went away and hid your talent in the ground. See, you have what is yours.'

26 "But his master answered and said to him, 'You wicked, lazy slave, you knew that I reap where I did not sow and gather where I scattered no *seed*. 27 Then you ought to have put my money in the bank, and on my arrival I would have received my *money* back with interest. 28 Therefore take away the talent from him, and give it to the one who has the ten talents.'

We must learn to manage all aspects of our life – spiritual, financial, relational, emotional, and physical. Management requires a plan, goals and a vision (see previous chapters and chapter to follow).

Do not just stumble through life! Choose to be proactive and manage your life so that you can benefit not only for yourself, but for those you love and those whom you will serve. Remember, God expects us to be good managers of the things he has entrusted us with (family, job, possessions etc.)

<u>Homework</u> – examine all the areas of life and determine if you need to be doing a better job of "management". Work with more experience people to help you in this area of your life.

Proverbs 6:6-11
Go to the ant, O sluggard,
Observe her ways and be wise,
Which, having no chief,
Officer or ruler,
Prepares her food in the summer
And gathers her provision in the harvest.
How long will you lie down, O sluggard?
When will you arise from your sleep?
"A little sleep, a little slumber,
A little folding of the hands to rest" –
Your poverty will come in like a vagabond
And your need like an armed man.

Ephesians 5:15-16
Therefore be careful how you walk, not as unwise men but as wise, making the most of your time, because the days are evil.

Experience

"Experience is the best teacher" **- Unknown**

"Experience is the teacher of all things." **Julius Caesar**

<u>Definition - Experience</u> - practical knowledge, skill, or practice derived from direct observation of or participation in events or in a particular activity

My son was complaining the other day about making minimum wage at one of his jobs (he has three jobs). I explained to him the following:

If you have minimum education, minimum skills and minimum experience, then you should expect minimum wages. An employer is only willing to pay more for experience, higher education and increased skills.

Think of a typical All American high school football players and a typical All American college football player. All other things being equal, who is more likely to be drafted by an NFL team? The player with more experience of course.

In most instances in life, there is not a good substitute for experience. I can remember when I went on my first college recruiting trip with my company and I was only 26 years old. I asked the more experienced recruiter how I would know the exceptional candidate from the average and his response was "after two 12 hour days of recruiting interviews, you will know". I thought he was crazy, but he was right!

When I interviewed my first student, she blew me out of the water and I was very impressed. However, the next student sounded just like the first and then it was a long line of interviews that all sounded the same. It was not until the end of the second day that one and only one candidate stood out from all the rest. I had to experience all of the other interviews to know he was the one.

However, it is not always necessary to "experience" something to learn the lesson.

I tell my children that they can choose wisdom or the can choose experience – the choice is theirs. You do not have to experience drugs to know they are bad for you. You do not have to experience alcohol to know it will make you drunk. You do not have to experience sex to know there is a risk of infection and or pregnancy. In some instances, you do not need the experience to learn the lesson. You can just choose wisdom

Homework – Gain experience in those things that have lasting effects (work, school, leadership, relationships etc.) and choose wisdom over experience when it comes to the "pleasures of this world".

Deuteronomy 1:15
So I took the heads of your tribes, wise and experienced men, and appointed them heads over you, leaders of thousands and of hundreds, of fifties and of tens, and officers for your tribes.

Leadership

"A leader is one who knows the way, goes the way, and shows the way." **John C. Maxwell**

<u>Definition - Leadership</u> - the power or ability to lead other people

If no one is following you, then you are not a leader!

Lead, follow or get out of the way! Simple, yet very profound. Many people stand in the middle of the road and choose to neither lead nor follow. They become obstacles for others and usually get run over.

Leadership is about responsibility and direction (many times it is also about casting a vision – see next chapter).

A great leader is one who builds a great team, but also achieves their goals and objectives.

John Maxwell has several great books on leadership that I would highly recommend:

Developing the Leader Within You
Developing the Leaders Around You
The 21 Irrefutable Laws of Leadership
Leadership 101: What Every Leader Needs to Know
The 5 Levels of Leadership: Proven Steps to Maximize Your Potential

If you are a parent, then you are in a leadership position whether you like it or not! Do not shrink from your responsibilities, but grow into them and seek out mentors and relationships that will help you become the leader you need to be.

<u>Homework</u> – take the opportunity this year to lead a project, group or organization. Stop being a follower and become a leader. Read some of John Maxwell's books and apply the lessons learned.

Exodus 18:21

Furthermore, you shall select out of all the people able men who fear God, men of truth, those who hate dishonest gain; and you shall place these over them as leaders of thousands, of hundreds, of fifties and of tens.

Luke 22:26

But it is not this way with you, but the one who is the greatest among you must become like the youngest, and the leader like the servant.

Vision

"*The most pathetic person in the world is someone who has sight, but has no vision.*" **Helen Keller**

"*Vision without execution is just hallucination.*" **Henry Ford**

<u>Definition - Vision</u> - a thought, concept, or object formed by the imagination

If you do not see it before you see it, you will never see it. This sounds profound, but it is really quite simple. It is about vision.

Vision is something that you have to see in your mind first and build out in your brain. Having a vision is also about having confidence in yourself that the vision is based in reality and can be executed.

Children are great at casting visions and thinking BIG! It is adults who think small and get distracted with everything that can and does go wrong. Take the time to listen to your child's dreams and visions. Help them to achieve these dreams! One of the greatest tasks I hold dear as a father is to be a dream maker and not a dream taker!

I will share with you one of the visions I have for my children.

My vision is for my children to see the world through God's eyes through mission work on all six continents by the time they finish high school. I want my children experience worship in different languages and cultures and yet see all these people serving the same God!

To make that a practical reality, we have to start in the 6th or 7th grade. Last year my daughter Sarah went on a mission trip with my Bride in North America. This year she went with me to Africa on a mission trip. Next year she is going to Europe on a mission trip. Here is the plan for the following years:

9th Grade – Mission trip to South America
10th Grade – Mission Trip to Asia
11th/12th Grade – Mission trip to Australia

What is your vision?

Homework – read the life biography of Thomas Edison or Henry Ford. While both of these men certainly had their foibles and imperfections, they were able to cast a vision and more importantly, make it a reality.

Proverbs 29:18
Where there is no vision, the people are unrestrained,
But happy is he who keeps the law.

Confidence

"Confidence doesn't come out of nowhere. It's a result of something... hours and days and weeks and years of constant work and dedication." **Roger Staubach**

Confidence is contagious. So is lack of confidence. **Vince Lombardi**

<u>Definition - Confidence</u> - a feeling or belief that you can do something well or succeed at something

How does one build confidence?   In one's self or in others?

It begins with unconditional love! Unconditional love does not judge, but seeks to build up and edify.   Unconditional love does not hold a grudge or remember the slight.   Unconditional love allows us to view the whole person and not just the sum of their parts.

To build confidence you have to create an atmosphere of love and respect.

To build confidence, you have to be willing to fail and let others fail.   That sounds crazy, but it is in the trying and the effort that you gain the confidence to complete a task.   Nobody will master a task the first time, it must be practiced again and again.

Here is an easy example of confidence building.

Did anybody learn to ride a bike the very first time?   I doubt it!   Learning to ride a bike began with training wheels on the bike to get the feel for the bike and understand the mechanics.   It was safe and the child became confident in the themselves and comfortable with the bike.   After some time, the training wheels came off.

This is when the parent comes alongside the child and holds the bike while they get on and start pedaling.   What inevitably happens?   The child falls down and tears are usually quick to follow.

No reasonable parent would stop the bike riding after one fall and quit and say, "well, my child will never learn to ride a bike".   Of course not! Below is what we usually say:

- "If you fall down, you just have to keep getting back up on the bike"

- "I know You can do it"

- "I believe in you"

- "You are making great progress, keep trying"

It is all about building confidence in an atmosphere of love and trust.   This is one simple example, but it holds true for all the things we try to teach our children and it should hold true for ourselves as well.

Fall down three times, but get up four!

Homework – build your confidence by believing in yourself and completing a hard task you have set before you. The key is working hard and actually completing the task.

Proverbs 3:26
For the Lord will be your confidence
And will keep your foot from being caught.

Psalm 71:5
For You are my hope; O Lord God, You are my confidence from my youth.

Psalm 78:7

That they should put their confidence in God And not forget the works of God, But keep His commandments,

Hebrews 4:16

Therefore let us draw near with confidence to the throne of grace, so that we may receive mercy and find grace to help in time of need.

Communication

"Communication is a skill that you can learn. It's like riding a bicycle or typing. If you're willing to work at it, you can rapidly improve the quality of every part of your life." **Brian Tracy**

<u>Definition - Communication</u> - the act or process of using words, sounds, signs, or behaviors to express or exchange information or to express your ideas, thoughts, feelings, etc., to someone else

How many types of communication are there? Certainly most people will think of verbal communication, but the definition above does an excellent job of describing the many different ways to communicate.

As a matter of fact, non-verbal communication is much more important to conveying your message than the actual words you use.

We have found in our marriage and with our children that we can NEVER let there be a time when we are NOT communicating. We know that the stiff silence or the cold shoulder only lets pain fester and become deadly. Instead, we continue to talk and communicate (even when it is painful). We have found that it is better to keep the lines of communication open, than to shut them down.

I had a period in my life where I did not communicate with my parents or siblings for many years! It was foolish and stupid on my part and I should have been proactive in reaching out to them. However, I let my pride get in the way and my father died before we ever spoke again.

Please do not let your pride get in the way of communicating with the ones you love.

<u>Homework</u> - is there someone in your life that you need to communicate with? Take the time to reach out to them today. Do not hesitate.

James 1:
This you know, my beloved brethren. But everyone must be quick to hear, slow to speak and slow to anger;

Proverbs 15:1
A gentle answer turns away wrath,
But a [a]harsh word stirs up anger.

Ephesians 4:29
Let no unwholesome word proceed from your mouth, but only such a word as is good for edification according to the need of the moment, so that it will give grace to those who hear.

Proverbs 25:11
Like apples of gold in settings of silver
Is a word spoken in right circumstances.

Yes

"The oldest, shortest words - 'yes' and 'no' - are those which require the most thought." **Pythagoras**

<u>Definition - Yes</u> - used to give a positive answer or reply to a question, request, or offer

Yes can be the best answer you ever give and it can be the worst answer you every give. It all depends on the wisdom and insight that goes into that answer.

I find that when most people are asked to take on additional tasks or responsibilities in the church, they will answer "yes" without any thought or foresight. They are afraid to say no because they are afraid they will upset or offend the person asking. It is great if they say yes and meant it and understood the responsibilities and consequences, but invariably the yes leads to frustration for both parties.

I love the quote above, because it is so very true, but few people follow this advice. We have tried to instill in our children that they should answer YES or NO and not equivocate! Many people will put off a hard decision by answering MAYBE. I have learned that MAYBE just means NO!! It somcone tells me MAYBE, then I put them in the NO column.

By the way - I am very glad my Bride said "yes" to me all those many years ago when I asked her to marry me.

<u>Homework</u> - Let your yes be yes! Do not equivocate.

Matthew 5:37
But let your statement be, 'Yes, yes' or 'No, no'; anything beyond these is of evil.

No

"The art of leadership is saying no, not saying yes. It is very easy to say yes." **Tony Blair**

<u>Definition - No</u> - used to give a negative answer or reply to a question, request, or offer

I am usually predisposed to saying no! As a matter of fact, I do not have any issues with telling people no. My biggest issue is with myself and the reason that I answer no.

The older I get the more circumspect I become with why I do or do not do things. I have found that many times when I am saying no to something it is because of selfishness in my own life.

I was recently asked to take a leadership position at church and after much thought and prayer I said "no". Without going into details, I am in a season of life that would not allow me to give this role the time, energy and effort that is required to do the job right.

The one thing that I have found to be very true is that I try to never make the YES or NO answers for my family without being aligned with my Bride. She always brings such good wisdom and thought into her decision making process and invariably she also brings a perspective that I have not considered.

<u>Homework</u> - Let your no be no! Do not equivocate.

Matthew 5:37
But let your statement be, 'Yes, yes' or 'No, no'; anything beyond these is of evil.

Start

"Start where you are. Use what you have. Do what you can."
Arthur Ashe

"A journey of a thousand miles begins with a single step." **Lao-tzu**

<u>Definition - Start</u> - to begin doing something

There is the story about Napoleon and a conversation he had with his generals concerning his army.

Napoleon saw a grand vision for his army and he wanted them to be able to move across the country in an efficient manner.   To that end, he commanded his generals to plant trees along all the lanes so that the troops could march in the shade.   His generals balked at the idea and told him that it would take 80 years for the trees to grow and create the kind of shade that he had envisioned.   Napoleon turned to his general and said "well then, you should start planting them today".

Many people are paralyzed by the thought of starting (the planning, obstacles, the work involved, etc.).   But Napoleon knew that it was important just to get started. Knowing when to start is just a critical as actually getting started itself.

Do not be like those who put off until tomorrow what they should be doing today.

Is there something in your life that you need to start doing?   Study, work, exercise, apology, investing?

<u>Homework</u> - What is keeping you from starting you tasks? You know what you need to do. Just do it and get started today.

Luke 7:6
Now Jesus started on His way with them; and when He was not far from the house, the centurion sent friends, saying to Him, "Lord, do not trouble Yourself further, for I am not worthy for You to come under my roof;

Stop

"When you find yourself in a hole, stop digging." **Will Rogers**

<u>Definition - Stop</u> - to not do something that you have been doing before : to not continue doing something

Just as in the previous chapter I talked about knowing when to start, it is just as important to know when to stop!

Think about STOP signs. They are not put at an intersection for decoration. They are put there for a reason.

Why is the STOP sign there? To keep you from dangerous situations.

Perhaps the road is at a dead end. Perhaps it is a busy intersection of roads and you would be in danger if you did not stop and survey our surroundings first and determine when it is safe to cross or proceed.

Learning when to stop starts at a young age. Unfortunately many parents are reluctant to teach their children the value of stopping.

I heard the story of a mother who never taught her son the value of stopping. When he was a toddler, he would get away from his mother and she would tell him to stop or there would be trouble. He would look at her and keep going and she never brought the "trouble" or discipline for his disobedience. He continued with this pattern of running away from his mother and not stopping when she yelled at him.

One day they were walking down the street and he pulled away from her and ran into the road. The mother yelled for him to stop, and he just smiled and kept on going. He was struck by a car and killed. It was not the drivers fault. The mother was completely culpable for the actions of her son.

Are there STOP signs in your life that you need to be paying attention to?

Is your conscience yelling STOP? Are people who love you telling you to STOP? Are you listening?

Homework - is there anything in your life that you need to stop doing? Be brave enough to admit you need to stop and get help from loved ones if necessary.

Acts 8:38
And he ordered the chariot to stop; and they both went down into the water, Philip as well as the eunuch, and he baptized him.

Money

"A Penny Saved is a Penny Earned" **Benjamin Franklin**

"There are three conversions a person needs to experience: The conversion of the head, the conversion of the heart, and the conversion of the pocketbook." **Martin Luther**

<u>**Definition - Money**</u> - something (such as coins or bills) used as a way to pay for goods and services and to pay people for their work

There are over 500 verses in the bible on faith, 500 on prayer and over 2,000 on money! This is definitely a word that God thought was important to talk about.

Money is a tool. Money is neither positive nor negative. Money is not evil or good. Money is neutral.

People are evil or good, people are positive or negative. Money is neutral.

Is there such a thing as too much money? For many people the answer is yes! They come to trust in the money and what it can bring instead of trusting in God in what he can do.

How do you view money in your life? It is a tool for good? Or is it a tool for selfishness? How often do you bless others with your money? Do you talk to your children about money? Do you and your spouse talk about money in a positive and constructive way? Do you control your money, or does your money control you?

<u>Homework</u> - Study the two verses at the end of this chapter and contemplate them for a week.   Review you banking and credit accounts and see how well they line up with God's perspective on money.

Matthew 6:24

"No one can serve two masters; for either he will hate the one and love the other, or he will be devoted to one and despise the other. You cannot serve God and wealth.

1 Timothy 6:10

For the love of money is a root of all sorts of evil, and some by longing for it have wandered away from the faith and pierced themselves with many grief's.

Invest

"You can tell the measure of a person by how they invest their time, talents and treasure". **Anonymous**

<u>Definition - Invest</u> - to commit (money) in order to earn a financial return
2: to make use of for future benefits or advantages <invested her time wisely>
3: to involve or engage especially emotionally <were deeply invested in their children's lives

Investing is not just about money. Just as the quote above say, it is about how you choose to invest your time, talents and treasures. It is about being intentional about all aspects of your life and very circumspect about where you will invest.

If you were to invest $10,000 in stocks and bonds, my guess is that you would have some expectation of a positive return over time. Perhaps in 10 years the $10,000 would become $25,000. You make the investment because you want to see a positive return

Most of us have limited resources and when we have limited resources we do not want to waste them. I would argue that the most valuable and yet most limited resource these days is our time!

Whether rich or poor, big or small, we all only have 24 hours in each day. When a day has passed, we cannot redeem that time. It is gone!

Have you given thought as to how you will invest your time? Whose life will you invest in? Will it be a positive investment?

My Bride and I had the opportunity to make an investment in a young couple from our church.   They approached us about doing some premarital counseling and after some prayer and thought we agreed.   It was a great opportunity for us to make an investment in their future marriage and help them to achieve a positive, long-term results.

As a family, we financially support a number of missionaries and many friends and neighbors who go on short term mission trips. Only on the other side of eternity will we be able to see the results of some of these investments.

To be effective in your investments, you must be very intentional as to when, where and how you will invest.

Homework - look at your time, talents and treasures this week and see if you are on track to get a positive return on your investments or not.

2 Corinthians 9:6

Now this I say, he who sows sparingly will also reap sparingly, and he who sows bountifully will also reap bountifully.

Debt

"There are no shortcuts when it comes to getting out of debt."
Dave Ramsey

Polonius:
Neither a borrower nor a lender be;
For loan oft loses both itself and friend,
And borrowing dulls the edge of husbandry.
This above all: to thine own self be true,
And it must follow, as the night the day,
Thou canst not then be false to any man.
Hamlet Act 1, scene 3,

Definition - Debt - an amount of money that you owe to a person, bank, company, etc.

We hate debt with a passion! Let me say this again, we hate debt with a passion!!   We have come to a place where the only debt we have is our home mortgage and it is on a very fast track to be paid off! We will never borrow money again.

I read a statistic the other day that the average college student comes away from college with over $25,000 in debt and that total student loan debt is over $1 trillion!! We have become convinced that one of the greatest gifts we can give our children is have them come out of college debt free.

How do we do this? Sacrifice and save! We drive old cars, we shop at goodwill, and we almost never eat out.   We started saving for college when our children were born and most importantly, they have "skin in the game". They have had jobs since they were 16 and have been responsible for almost all of their expenses (gas, car, insurance, phone, clothing, etc.).

We have taught our children to live on a budget and live within their means, and we practice what we preach.

We talk to our children about the evils of debt and how you become a slave to it and how it can ruin your relationship with others and cause undue friction in your life.

We hate debt!   We want you and your family to hate debt as well.

Homework - If you are in debt trouble, I strongly encourage you to connect with Dave Ramsey at daveramsey.com.   He has some incredible and practical advice.   Learn to hate debt and learn to develop financial discipline.

Proverbs 13:22
A good man leaves an inheritance to his children's children,
And the wealth of the sinner is stored up for the righteous.

Romans 13:8
Owe nothing to anyone except to love one another; for he who loves his neighbor has fulfilled the law.

Proverbs 22:7
The rich rules over the poor, And the borrower becomes the lender's slave.

Surprise

"The backbone of surprise is fusing speed with secrecy. "
Carl von Clausewitz

<u>Definition - Surprise</u> - an unexpected event, piece of information, etc

It may be a surprise to you that surprise is one of my top 100 words.

This is a wonderful word that I weave into my life all the time. I talk to my children and tell them I have a surprise for them. A surprise means that we are going to do something fun, but I have no idea what and adventure lies before us.

This is so much fun, because I am usually a very intentional and meticulous planner. However, I have found that there is a lot of fun in a surprise and what it might bring.

I love to surprise my Bride by bringing her flowers on a random day or decorating her car with "I Love You" notes.

I love to surprise my children by just loading up in the car and taking them for a treat and not telling them where we are going.

This is such a great word and it can bring joy to your life and the ones you love.

To practice what I preach, as soon as I finish this chapter I am taking my kids out for a surprise treat!

<u>Homework</u> - build some surprises into your week!

Laugh

William Makepeace Thackeray

<u>Definition: Laugh</u> - to show that you are happy or that you think something is funny by smiling and making a sound from your throat

I love when our house if filled with laughter! There is nothing more wonderful than to hear laughter coming from our kitchen and then going there to investigate and join in the fun.

We have a family of six, so it is rare that everybody is in a good mood and enjoying life. Usually one of us has some sort of trial we are dealing with. But on those occasions when we do gather together to laugh and share, it is truly amazing.

It is the also the rare day when nobody is laughing at all! We love to laugh! Not just a short chuckle, but a good "belly laugh". My sons are both natural comedians and love any audience and the opportunity to bring a smile and laugh to our faces.

Is there laughter in your house? In your family? In your life? I hope you are not one of those miserable people who never laughs or enjoys life.

<u>Homework</u> - Find a good movie comedy to watch and let laughter fill your house. Look at some funny YouTube videos together as a family. Take the opportunity to create an atmosphere of laughter in you home.

Ecclesiastes 3:4
A time to weep and a time to laugh; A time to mourn and a time to dance.

Proverbs 17:22

A joyful heart is good medicine,
But a broken spirit dries up the bones

Proverbs 15:13

A joyful heart makes a cheerful face,
But when the heart is sad, the spirit is broken.

Curiosity

"It is a miracle that curiosity survives formal education."
Albert Einstein

<u>Definition:</u> <u>Curiosity</u> - the desire to learn or know more about something or someone

I am curious about so many things. I can remember growing up as a young boy and wondering how things worked. I would take my toys and small appliances apart just to see the how they worked (and then I tried to put them back together again, I was only marginally successful).

My son Jonathan is definitely the most curious of all my children.   He is constantly asking "why" or "what".   It can seem annoying at times, but I realize he is trying to synthesize the world through the lens of an 11 year old.   We have fostered curiosity in all of our children and in our marriage as well.   We are constantly asking "why" and "what" and encouraging our children to do the same.   This is how we learn.

Curiosity has led us on many cool adventures and some very neat discoveries.   I cannot imagine life without curiosity and questions. I encourage you to step out of your comfort zone and be more curious about the wonderful world around you.   You never know what you might discover.

<u>Homework</u>: - Take the time this week to seek out information about something you are curious about and share it with your family.

<u>Proverbs 25:2</u>
It is the glory of God to conceal a matter,
But the glory of kings is to search out a matter.

Fun

"Fun is good." **Dr. Seuss**

"If a man insisted always on being serious, and never allowed himself a bit of fun and relaxation, he would go mad or become unstable without knowing it" **Herodotus**

<u>Definition: **Fun**</u> - an enjoyable or amusing time

I am sitting in my basement writing this chapter with my son Jonathan. He is very curious about my book and wanted to know if I had put the word FUN in the book.

Jonathan is 11 years old and the world for him right now is all about fun. We just finished coloring Easter eggs and there was a huge smile on his face the whole time we were doing it. His older sister Sarah Grace did not want to help out (she is 13 now) because it seemed childish. However, after a few minutes of seeing how much fun Jonathan was having, she jumped right in and started coloring eggs as well.

As a family we are always trying to build fun into our day and week. As you have seen in earlier chapters, I use the word intentional a lot! It is ok to be intentional about having fun and planning fun things in your life.

Some of the fun things we plan:

- North Georgia State Fair
- Vacation to the beach
- Going to the $1.00 theater
- Visiting the Humane Society to see the dogs and cats
- Hiking

There are also opportunities each day to just have fun at home.   Jonathan likes to "wrestle" at night and Sarah Grace like to read stories together.

The main point is that as a family, fun is something we build into our lives and into our schedule.

I do not want to be one of those miserable people from my company who brags about working all the time and never using all their vacation (as if this was some badge of honor).   We never know how much time we have left here on earth, so cherish each day and build some fun into your schedule.

Homework - Take time this week to look at your calendar and build some fun into your schedule.   It does not have to be something that cost any money, it is more about the intentional time commitment.

Memories

"The heart of marriage is memories; and if the two of you happen to have the same ones and can savor your reruns, then your marriage is a gift from the gods." **Bill Cosby**

<u>Definition - Memory</u> - something that is remembered

Memories are interesting things to consider. There are good memories and bad memories. I want to focus this chapter on the good memories and how we go about intentionally creating them.

Can you create a memory? You sure can!

We create memories by intentionally scheduling time together as a family (or as a couple) because unless you are spending time together then it is pretty hard to create a shared memory.

My Bride and I get away for long weekends and regular dates together and have time to focus on one another and create some incredible memories.

Our family gets away each year on a family vacation (for us it is to the beach. Note that I use the word invest. We do not see family vacation time as a "cost" we see it as an investment. When it is viewed through that lens of thinking, then it helps prioritize how we save and spend money so we can invest in a vacation. Sometimes when money is tight, the length of the stay or the quality of the lodging may less than desired, but creating memories through a vacation is always a priority.

The point about creating memories is that you want to be around your family and loved ones enough that you can create memories. You just never know when the circumstances will offer the opportunity for a memory.

Some cool memories:

- Jonathan falling out of the raft as we were white water rafting.

- Jumping off a 30 foot cliff into the ocean with my daughter Hannah.

- Teaching my children to surf and building sand castles.

- Watching my oldest children jump out of a perfectly safe airplane.

- Getting caught in a severe thunderstorm while camping.

- Any campfire cooking hotdogs and sharing stories.

- Tour of New York City with Hannah & David

- Taking Sarah Grace to the Mall of America and her first plane trip.

All of these things were intentional scheduled time together where we were trying to create memories (and did).

You cannot redeem a single day that passes.   Take the opportunity to create memories with your loved ones.

Homework - Look at your calendar and schedule a family event that will help create a memory.

Proverbs 10:7
The memory of the righteous is blessed,
But the name of the wicked will rot.

Luke 2:
But Mary treasured all these things, pondering them in her heart.

Rest

"Take rest; a field that has rested gives a bountiful crop." **Ovid**

<u>Definition - Rest</u> - freedom from activity or labor

We take rest very seriously! My Bride has a running joke with me. She is constantly saying - "is it time to rest yet"?   She usually says this at a time when I am pushing forward and driving the family harder than I should.

I tend to be an all or nothing person. I work 12-18 hours per day for a while and then just crash.   I rest and then go at it again.   Definitely not the way to go about getting adequate rest.

As I spoke about in the chapter called HALT, I explained that being tired is one of the triggers for bad decisions. We have another rule that we live by - we never make any important decisions (especially financial) if we are tired.   We have gone to bed many times to sleep on decisions and more times than not, have changed our minds.

We purposefully rest on Sunday's after church!   A nap and no activities really gets us ready to face the new week and recharge our batteries. It was good enough for God and that is a pretty good example to follow.

On most weekends I turn off my work cell phone and work computer and do not do any work at all.   My mind needs a rest and break and I find that I am much more productive during the following week if I do not work on the weekends.

My Bride and I schedule time away with each other to refresh and recharge (usually 2-3 times per year for a long weekend). We have been taking family vacations every year since we have been married and see this not only as a time of rest but an opportunity to create lasting memories and pour ourselves deeply into each family member and focus on each other.

We have so many friends and family members who never seem to rest. They are in constant motion and go from activity to activity and miss the opportunity to just sit back and enjoy the life God has given us.

When was the last time you had time to form a cognitive thought?

Homework - if you have not made rest a habit or part of your life, then start this weekend and be very intentional about when you will rest.

Genesis 2:2-3
By the seventh day God completed His work which He had done, and He rested on the seventh day from all His work which He had done. Then God blessed the seventh day and sanctified it, because in it He rested from all His work which God had created and made.

Seasons

"If we had no winter, the spring would not be so pleasant; if we did not sometimes taste of adversity, prosperity would not be so welcome." **Anne Bradstreet**

<u>Definition - Season</u> - a time characterized by a particular circumstance or feature

I was speaking with my oldest daughter Hannah just the other day about the importance of understanding the seasons of life and situations. She is about to head off to a major University after spending two years at the local college. Her desire is to stay busy and be involved in a ton of activities.

She just got back from a mission trip to Africa over spring break and wanted to go to South Africa for the summer. Unfortunately, she has neither the time nor the money for such a worthy endeavor. Her heart is most definitely in the right place, but we had a long talk about her current need to focus on this season of college and completing the work there so that more doors will be opened for her in the future.

I explained that while I was working on my MBA I had a desire to go on missions trips and do many other things, but as a father of 4 and fully employed, I did not have the time or money to pursue this. It was a season that I was going through. That season passed a year ago and I just returned from my mission trip to Africa.

We had a season with small children and now we are in a season with grown children. We have enjoyed the challenges and opportunities that are presented in each season. We have found that you must try to get the most out of each season and not look to far into the future, lest you miss the blessing that are right in front of you.

What season are you in?   What are the challenges facing you? Seek God's wisdom and guidance in each season and try to enjoy the blessings and challenges as they are presented to you.   Know that seasons do not last forever (although some seem to never end) and God is faithful in all seasons.

<u>Homework</u> - examine your life and determine the season you are currently in.   How can you be a blessing to others during this season?   Look to others who have been through this season of life and seek their wisdom and guidance.

2 Timothy 4:2

preach the word; be ready in season and out of season; reprove, rebuke, exhort, with great patience and instruction.

Ecclesiastes 3:1-9

There is an appointed time for everything. And there is a time for every event under heaven —

A time to give birth and a time to die;
A time to plant and a time to uproot what is planted.
A time to kill and a time to heal;
A time to tear down and a time to build up.
A time to weep and a time to laugh;
A time to mourn and a time to dance.
A time to throw stones and a time to gather stones;
A time to embrace and a time to shun embracing.
A time to search and a time to give up as lost;
A time to keep and a time to throw away.
A time to tear apart and a time to sew together;
A time to be silent and a time to speak.
A time to love and a time to hate;
A time for war and a time for peace.

Promise

"Our Lord has written the promise of resurrection, not in books alone, but in every leaf in springtime." **Martin Luther**

Promises are like babies: easy to make, hard to deliver.
Author Unknown

<u>Definition - Promise</u> a statement telling someone that you will definitely do something or that something will definitely happen in the future

Did you know there are over 1,200 promises in the Bible? I use the one promise below all the time with my children and with young couple that we are mentoring.

Ephesians 6:2-3
Honor your father and mother (which is the first commandment with a promise), so that it may be well with you, and that you may live long on the earth.

It is very comforting to me to know that God has made so many promises in His word and that He keeps His promises.

John 3:16
"For God so loved the world, that He gave His only begotten Son, that whoever believes in Him shall not perish, but have eternal life.

What an incredible promise to all of man kind! To God be the glory!!

What about use, we also make promises each and every day of the week.

- I promise to clean the garage out this weekend
- I promise to take the kids to the park
- I promise to take you on a date
- I promise to stop looking at pornography
- I promise to put the lid down on the toilet
- I promise to make it to your – ball game, musical, dance recital, etc.

Our spouse and our children are looking to us to see if we will keep these promises.

Every time you keep a promise you reinforce the value of that person to you. And conversely, you diminish their value when you do not keep your promise. Ultimately this is about trust! Can your family trust you and believe you are a person of your word.

Trust is such a foundational element of all relationships, that when you do not keep your promises, you are tearing down the foundation you are standing upon.

Homework: what promise have you broken that you can work on this week? Ask forgiveness and create a new path for the promises you will keep.

Deuteronomy 31:6
Be strong and courageous, do not be afraid or tremble at them, for the Lord your God is the one who goes with you. He will not fail you or forsake you.

Romans 10:9
that if you confess with your mouth Jesus as Lord, and believe in your heart that God raised Him from the dead, you will be saved;

Finish

"Finishing well requires tenacity, resolve, and integrity."
Allen Randolph

<u>Definition - Finish</u> - to reach the end of (something) : to stop doing (something) because it is completed

I intentionally wanted to end with this word.

I was at a funeral recently for a woman who was the mother of one of my close friends. Many people talked about the positive impact she had in their lives (both friends and family).   At the end, one of her sons came to the front and said "Mom finished well".

What a tribute to a faithful woman!

My pastor has consistently said over the years that he wants to "finish well".

Paul was speaking to his young disciple Timothy when he wrote the following:

<u>2 Timothy 4:7</u>
I have fought the good fight, I have finished the course, I have kept the faith;

It is my desire to finish well! I don't know when the finish line will be reached, so I need to constantly be striving as if the finish line is close.

<u>Homework</u> - we might not all start well, but praise God we can finish well. Begin working today, as if the finish line was very close. We never know how much time we will have.

Philippians 3:14
I press on toward the goal for the prize of the upward call of God in Christ Jesus.

Philippians 1:6
For I am confident of this very thing, that He who began a good work in you will perfect it until the day of Christ Jesus.

Final Thoughts

First, thank you so much for taking the time to read this book. It is my prayer that this has been a blessing to you and your family.

Secondly, if you have an opportunity to send me an e-mail with your thoughts, comments or suggestions, that would be very helpful.

paulbeersdorf@gmail.com

Finally - while there are over 1mm English words, I hope you take the time to add to this list and commit to creating your own list of words to live by.

Blessings to you and your family!

Paul Beersdorf

Appendix

In Alphabetical Order

www.ingramcontent.com/pod-product-compliance
Lightning Source LLC
Chambersburg PA
CBHW071528040426
42452CB00008B/923